T0194808

FAITHFUL

Stories of Trust, Courage, and Resilience

Paul R Alexander

WESTBOW
PRESS®
A DIVISION OF THOMAS NELSON
& ZONDERVAN

This book is a work of non-fiction. Unless otherwise noted, the author
and the publisher make no explicit guarantees as to the accuracy of
the information contained in this book and in some cases, names of
people and places have been altered to protect their privacy.

WestBow Press books may be ordered through booksellers or by contacting:

WestBow Press
A Division of Thomas Nelson & Zondervan
1663 Liberty Drive
Bloomington, IN 47403
www.westbowpress.com
844-714-3454

Because of the dynamic nature of the Internet, any web addresses or
links contained in this book may have changed since publication and
may no longer be valid. The views expressed in this work are solely those
of the author and do not necessarily reflect the views of the publisher,
and the publisher hereby disclaims any responsibility for them.

Any people depicted in stock imagery provided by Getty Images are
models, and such images are being used for illustrative purposes only.
Certain stock imagery © Getty Images.

ISBN: 978-1-6642-5746-7 (sc)
ISBN: 978-1-6642-5747-4 (hc)
ISBN: 978-1-6642-5745-0 (e)

Library of Congress Control Number: 2022902376

Print information available on the last page.

WestBow Press rev. date: 3/9/2022

CONTENTS

ENDORSEMENTS

God works in mysterious ways! In this story we repeatedly read about miracles when God provides and opens new doors. We also, time after time, meet ordinary men and women, passionate for the Kingdom and eager to serve. Is it God or men? The answer is YES? God in us! The marvellous story of Trinity Bible Collage shows the importance good training of Christian leadership. Training is about intelligent minds, passionate hearts, and skilled hands. All to the glory and service for God's kingdom.

Ulrik Josefsson, Prorector at Academy for Leadership and Theology, Sweden

This book will inspire, encourage and challenge you to greater faith! It's a story of God's divine direction in the lives of two amazing people - Drs Paul and Carol Alexander and an obscure Bible college named Trinity. If you've ever had a doubt that God still does the miraculous in the magnitude of pillars of fire and water from rocks, you'll not doubt again. This book is a Must Read!!

Rev. Stephen Schaible, District Superintendent South Dakota Assemblies of God, United States

This is an inspiring story commencing with a dream of coming change and concluding with a case for Christian higher education delivered within community. Dr Paul Alexander describes God calling him and his wife Carol to the Presidency of Trinity Bible College and the significant turnaround in its ministry as faithful people committed to support. It is an engaging account of struggle, progress, miracles, and fruitfulness. It is also a call to value and support Christian higher education.

Professor Stephen Fogarty, President of Alphacrucis College, Australia

Dr. Paul Alexander chronicles his and Dr. Carol's extraordinary call to Trinity and their leading through each phase of the school's restoration. He shares the unique pathway taken to repair the school's structures, reputation, and purpose, while weaving an account of God's miraculous provision throughout the journey. Dr. Paul champions the friends of Trinity, who sacrificially supported the restoration efforts at every turn. As a Trinity alumnus, I treasure this written testament of God's incredible activity and supernatural intervention. This book will encourage anyone who needs a fresh shot of hope and faith that God still speaks prophetically and provides for our needs in supernatural ways.

Kay Burnett, Director of AG Women, Assemblies of God National Office, United States

One of the compelling roles of a leader working in partnership with the Spirit of God is to restore, revive and renew. I first met Pastor Paul Alexander in Brisbane, Australia in 1992. From the moment I witnessed the ministry he was involved in, it was evident that restoration, revival, and renewal was a mandate with which he operated. That he has successfully carried out this mandate at Trinity Bible College and graduate school is of no surprise to those of us who know him. What a remarkable journey of faith and legacy he has pioneered in a new generation of graduates!

Pastor Glyn Barrett, Senior Pastor !Audacious Church, Great Britain
National Leader Assemblies of God, Great Britain
Co-Chair Empowered 21 Western Europe

It is with great enthusiasm that I recommend you invest the time & effort to read Dr Paul Alexander's story as captured in his recent release. You will be encouraged & challenged by how God will use a surrendered life. What's happening at Trinity is truly remarkable! This is a story that must be shared.

Rev. Mark Dean, District Superintendent Minnesota Assemblies of God, United States

The story of Trinity Bible College and Graduate School has been a miraculous one from the beginning. Under the remarkable leadership of Drs. Paul and Carol Alexander that miracle continues to unfold, now taking on wonderful new dimensions. You will find this recounting of that story inspiring, thought-provoking and faith-building.

Dr. James Bradford, Lead Pastor, Central Assemblies of God, Springfield, MO, United States

When Paul sent me the manuscript to read, I was riveted from page one. What a story! Full of stories, so well written. Honest and humble, a record for God's glory. A remarkable journey of God's faithfulness and supernatural provision through courageous vision and the obedience of faith – not without trials and testings, sacrifices and tears – with victories and amazing miracles. What shines brightest, for me, is not the story of Trinity Bible College *per se*, but the passion for God's Kingdom for all nations. Trinity has become a more than adequate vehicle to equip God's people, pastors, leaders and missionaries, around the world. Read and be inspired!

Alexander F Venter, Vineyard Pastor, Theologian, and Author, South Africa

Paul and Carol Alexander are visionary, transformational leaders whose call to Christian higher education has produced significant Kingdom influence that is trans-continental and inter-generational. In *Faithful: Stories of Faith, Courage, and Resilience,* Paul shares the challenges and achievements that frame the success story that is Trinity Bible College & Graduate School. This book is a testament to why Christian colleges and universities are important and will endure.

Michael J. Beals, Ph.D. President Vanguard University, United States

To know Paul and Carol is to love them! And their leadership journey at Trinity Bible College & Graduate School has been nothing short of remarkable. It really is a journey with the grace and goodness of God indelibly imprinted upon it. This book is an inspiring account that will stir your faith, forge new courage, and build deep resilience in these challenging times!

Byron Chicken, Group National Leader, AOG Group South Africa

FOREWORD TO
"FAITHFUL"

While waves of college closures spread across the United States, Trinity, in Ellendale, North Dakota, stands solid and even thrives. Under the inspired leadership of Dr. Paul Alexander, Trinity Bible College and Graduate School has become the great success in evangelical Christian higher education.

Trinity is like the state of North Dakota itself. Toughened by brutal winters of snow and ice, who could have imagined that such wealth lay just beneath its ground? Yet, in 2006 the Bakken formation was discovered and the whole region prospered with the North Dakota oil boom. Likewise, Trinity Bible College and Graduate School continues to surprise. Against all odds, and possibly outright opposition, Trinity has become fully accredited, and in a remarkable financial situation. Students, worldwide, study in its Graduate School which now fields 5 MAs and a PhD in Practical Theology. Undergraduate programs burst with creativity. The campus has been nearly completely renovated. New buildings grace the attractive grounds hinting at the substantial investment of friends who support the mission of the college. Well prepared graduates fan out across the Midwest and literally around the world from this small agrarian town. Under the leadership of Dr. Paul Alexander, this once "best kept secret" in evangelical Christian higher education has begun to catch worldwide attention.

In 1972, my late father, Dr. Roy Wead, was the President of Trinity Bible Institute. It was a small but growing center for preparing men and women for Pentecostal ministry housed in inadequate facilities in Jamestown, North Dakota.

Meanwhile, the Ellendale Branch of the University of North Dakota had experienced declining enrollment. The loss of two major buildings to a fire was the nail in the coffin. The institution was closed. What followed was a competitive scramble from hundreds of organizations across the country to purchase or take over the multi-million-dollar campus. The State was looking for a plan that would best benefit the community long term. My father submitted his plan. It would eventually require approval from the North Dakota legislature, the Governor's signature and a statewide referendum from the people, themselves. Eventually, the plan was accepted, and the 43-acre Ellendale campus was purchased by Trinity for $1. This remarkable story is the subject of a book I wrote in 1975, titled *The Great Multi-Million Dollar Miracle*.

How has this institution survived the wave of college closures across the nation and bucked the headwinds of liberal forces determined to undermine our Christian heritage? Dr. Paul Alexander, President of Trinity Bible College and Graduate School, outlines four reasons in this timely book.

Visionary leadership defies spiritual opposition. Since the 1948 founding of what is now Trinity Bible College and Graduate School, two of the greatest leaps ahead have been made under the visionary leadership of my father and Dr. Paul Alexander. Both were able to see what others could not see and guide the ship to that destination. A Christian college faces an unseen supernatural realm of opposition which is different than what any secular institution experiences. God-given vision coupled with the gift of faith has enabled Trinity to win the unseen battles.

The intentional creation of culture breathes life into weary organizations. To visit the campus is to sense the positive morale within the Trinity family. It is no accident; rather, a purposeful creation of building blocks of respect and honor that lead to a healthy environment. The daily social gathering of faculty, staff and administrators permeates the atmosphere with goodwill. Students who are molded by the community-based educational experience are prepared to duplicate healthy relationships wherever they go.

Ordinary spaces become hallowed places when dedicated to God's purpose. The biblical record is filled with incidents of common spaces being transformed into sacred and special places where God meets with humanity. It may be a high mountain, a threshing floor or an upper room, but the place will never be viewed the same and the person is changed forever. The Ellendale campus, under the leadership of Dr. Paul Alexander, is a place where thousands of students have discovered their destiny. It has become a hallowed space set aside for God's purpose.

The faithfulness of God and God's people overcome insurmountable odds. Trinity's story is ultimately the story of God's faithfulness. For decades faithful people carried the torch of a true Bible college couched in a rural setting that would reach not only it's region, but the nations. Times of disfavor, low enrollment and financial difficulties made it seem as though the Trinity would disappear. In his faithfulness, God seems to have placed his stamp of approval on this innovative institution for such a time as this – and perhaps for the decades to come.

Trinity's president, Dr. Alexander, is also the president of the Assemblies of God Alliance for Higher Education. While acknowledging the place of online education, he makes a passionate case for campus-based education. The value of life transformation that takes place in community defies a price tag. He maintains that Trinity's remote location uniquely positions it to be precisely what many students need to foster character and spiritual formation.

I love this book! Dr. Paul Alexander is an inspiration. My father, Roy Wead, would be so grateful and impressed by his leadership. Dad loved North Dakota. He was always bragging on the sunshine, declaring it to be a "typical North Dakota day." At some point you may visit Trinity Bible College and Graduate School to see the great work that Dr. Paul Alexander is doing. Hopefully, you will visit on one of those "typical North Dakota days!"

Doug Wead sadly passed away December 10, 2021.

PREFACE

I write these closing words as I gaze across our beautiful, but windswept campus. It is just a few weeks until Christmas, and the North Dakota winter has arrived in full force. Teams of staff and students have decorated the halls for the holidays, and the glimmer of warm, colored lights fill several windows.

It is this stark and remote location that confuses many. I suppose I would not have chosen a small town in rural North Dakota as the obvious location for a thriving Bible college and graduate school. But this is where the institution known as Trinity Bible College has taken root and is now thriving. In fact, this single institution has trained and educated people for decades. We get to meet these amazing people and hear their stories. Each one is a living defiance of the narrative that a Bible college in a small town is not viable. It is not only viable, but also a constant testimony to a faithful God whose ways are above finding out.

My heart is warmed as I survey this wonderful campus. New buildings, beautifully restored places and corridors filled with the happy chatter of hundreds of students. It all speaks to me of the amazing God whom Carol and I committed to serve nearly five decades ago. Through every season he has been faithful.

May this story continue to be written. Join with me in praying that the dreams and visions expressed throughout this book will become a reality. And now it remains for me to pray that you, my friend, will experience this same faithful God. In your life, in your need, in your family and in your future may He be faithful to you. Let us join our stories together in declaring how good our God is.

ACKNOWLEDGEMENTS

It is often said that it takes a village to educate a single student. The same is true when it comes to writing a book like this.

My sweetest life friend, coworker and wife, Carol, deserves first mention. Her steadfast commitment to God, me and God's work speaks more loudly than any story recorded here of the faithfulness of God. She has been my rock and strength through each season of life. Thank you is not adequate. I love you, Carol, with all my heart.

The names of many generous people run through this book. These stewards of God's resources are worthy of yet another mention. Gerry and Mary Schoonbee, you trusted a 28-year-old with a dream. It was you who began the journey that has now resulted in the army of kind and generous people, many referenced in this book, who have joined us in this great calling of training and educating men and women. The hundreds who have sown into our lives over many years, though not specifically mentioned, are remembered with gratitude.

My indefatigable executive assistant Jessica Saylor must take credit for helping get this book into a publishable state. For her many hours of labor and seemingly effortless use of technology that is far beyond my skill set, I am very grateful. Likewise, David and Rose Bennett labored for hours in proofreading the text. The Trinity story is incomplete without a special mention of this amazing couple. To them both, thank you.

The Board of Trustees under the capable leadership of Superintendent Stephen Schaible made the publishing of this book possible. As a result of their generosity, I can make this book available on the basis of a donation rather than a sale.

All proceeds from this book will find their way into the Trinity Bible College and Graduate School Endowment Fund. May this resource serve many generations of future students well.

Finally, to the great people of this Upper Midwest region – pastors, District Superintendents, District Youth Directors, and multiple people spread far and wide - thank you. You have welcomed us and made us one of your own. Our lives will forever have the imprint of the beautiful people of the Upper Midwest and the faithful God that they reflect.

INTRODUCTION

This book was written for many reasons. Fundamentally, it was an effort to record the extraordinary faithfulness of God in the life of a long-standing and noble institution. I wanted to be sure that the historical record was kept so that future generations can remember, and hopefully be wise stewards of this treasure we know as Trinity Bible College and Graduate School.

But the reasons are also much more textured. I took advantage of the opportunity afforded through the writing of this book to reflect upon our personal journey. Little has been written about Africa School of Missions and its extraordinary impact upon mission mobilization in South Africa especially in the 1990's and the early part of this millennium. Because this formed so much of the basis for our own commitment to ministry and missionary training it was important to include a brief reference to the founding of Africa School of Missions. However, it was extremely satisfying knowing that, if only in a few brief paragraphs, this remarkable story is not lost. It would be a worthwhile project indeed to write further on ASM and its impact. I privately hope that one of our PhD candidates might one day consider this project.

Another layer in this textured story is the appeal for the role of the Bible college in our contemporary church world. Some of the most significant advances of church movements in the late nineteenth and early twentieth centuries were undoubtedly helped by the role of the Bible institute movement. In fact, it is almost impossible to exclude the role of the academy in almost every era of church history. The current rapid expansion of the church in the two-thirds world cannot be divorced from the hunger for learning that these churches produce in their emerging leaders. Bible colleges have mushroomed around the globe and are most prevalent where there is quantifiable and significant church growth. I really do not want to sound defensive of Trinity alone. Rather, I am hoping to provoke church leaders nationally to reconsider some of the training models that the church has adopted. While some have obviously good effect, others need careful evaluation. Looking back at a lifetime of ministry training, I am more certain than ever that theology is taught as much around the lunch table and in late night discussions in dorm rooms as it is in the classroom. Will future generations judge us harshly for not facilitating this communal form of training and educating? It is a futile effort to try to underestimate the impact of community upon faith. In a post-COVID world most pastors have developed a clear polemic for the importance of the gathered church. This book is unapologetically written with the same appeal for the gathering of young leaders into learning communities. Is it possible that this book could provoke a discussion that could lead to a new Bible college movement across the United States?

Further peeling back the layers of this textured narrative, it will become evident to the reader that connected learning environments need the support of multiple friends. Common wisdom as found in the multiple books that have been written about faith-based institutions suggest that a healthy college is supported by about 80% from student revenue. In other words, tuition and other fees cover four out of every five dollars needed to support the institution. The remainder is income derived from donations and endowment funds. People dissect these numbers still further and complicated formulae are produced to determine policy such as maximum debt loads for institutions, the introduction of new programs and campus development. It is a sad reality that few colleges with a strong ministry preparation focus enjoy even this level of financial support. At Trinity our immensely kind donors have helped us achieve this level of financial health and then some. But the message that I am seeking to communicate cannot be blurred by this wonderful reality. Put simply, ministry training institutes need many generous friends. I would go so far as to predict that the day is not far away when we will need to raise up to 50% of the costs of running an institution, especially one that has ministry and missionary training as its primary focus and mission.

Multiple factors will determine this shift that I predict. In the US, the regulatory climate will not favor any level of government or even business support. Tax incentives will be eroded, and in some cases, any training program committed to training ministers and missionaries will likely face unprecedented headwinds. This means that this book is timely in influencing an ever-larger group of committed Christian people to prioritize a reasonable amount of their charitable giving to scholarship funds, capital projects and general fund activities in ministry training institutions. The ministry departments of our larger universities should not be excluded when speaking about this level of generosity. In acknowledging the extreme kindness of friends who have helped us prove the faithfulness of God at Trinity, this book is equally a challenge to all people of faith to reconsider their giving to ministry training enterprises. Likewise, every local church should without hesitation include the financial support of ministry training as a part of its budget. Even a cursory glance across the ecclesial landscape will show that the pipeline of ministers is almost empty. Church after church is finding it difficult to find someone to fill their pulpit. I hope this book is a gentle, yet forthright, reminder that we have likely failed at a systemic level in providing for the next generation of godly preachers, pastors and missionaries.

Finally, a thematic thread throughout this book is a call to Christian ministry. If we take the New Testament narrative seriously, read church history carefully and evaluate the incredible role of faith-filled communities in our society, it should lead to one conclusion. That is that men and women are called by God, set aside for ministry, supported by the church and released into Christ-honoring years of service. May the number of these heroic members of the army of the meek increase dramatically in the next decade. May the iron-sharpening-iron impact of the academy produce people of great character who refuse to bend or bow to the pressures of culture. May many arise and be prepared to serve anywhere, anytime, no matter the cost. It is on the shoulders of such courageous men and women throughout the centuries that the world-wide Church has been built. It is these who have served the poor, the orphan and the widow. It is these who educated millions through mission schools and cared for whole regions through clinics and hospitals.

This book is not for sale. It is freely given with the hope that it will provoke a response. The most immediate response is my desire to build a sizeable endowment fund at Trinity Bible College and Graduate School. But as the book's message is textured, so I anticipate will be the response of the readers. Perhaps this book will provoke you and your family to support a Bible college student. Perhaps a discussion will start at a local meeting of ministers about the need for a future Bible college. Whatever the reading of this book provokes, may it result in the great and strong name of our Lord Jesus being proclaimed more widely through preachers, pastors, missionaries, schoolteachers and many others. As our mission statement says so well: "so that people everywhere will hear the Good News and see Christ's love demonstrated through acts of kindness."

Paul R Alexander, PhD
Ellendale, ND
Christmas 2021

CHAPTER ONE

The Dream

It was a most unusual and early start to my day. Over forty years earlier I had married my sweetheart the week after we had graduated from college. I never doubted that she was both totally committed to being a Christ follower and was undoubtedly passionate about this.

But this was different. She was pushing on my shoulder and asking me to wake up. I mumbled something and asked her to go back to sleep. It was, after all, only about five o'clock. Before I am judged too harshly for my insensitivity, I must defend myself.

Carol was talking about a dream that she was convinced was God communicating to her. Although we knew that God used dreams to speak to people in the Bible and probably subsequently, we had never experienced divine guidance by means of one. So, being rudely awakened at an unearthly hour in order to hear my wife talk about a dream was not exactly what I wanted. I suggested that she go back to sleep and turned my back.

At breakfast Carol was desperately wanting to share the content of her dream with me. She insisted that it was a vivid dream and different than any other she had had previously. Again, I was resistant. I did not want the routine of my life to be interrupted. I had served God long enough to know that He is deeply involved in our everyday lives. I also could tell multiple stories of God's leading and guidance over the years. But a dream from apparently nowhere was not what I wanted that day.

At the time of the dream, Carol and I were leading the Assemblies of God College and Graduate School in the United Kingdom. The College was actually our alma mater. It was situated in a quintessential little English village called Mattersey in northern Nottinghamshire. The College occupied a grand old house called Mattersey Hall. Its origins went back to a 17th century manor house, and it had been substantially and grandly added to by a newly rich industrialist in the late Victorian period. During the Second World War a new building had been added to the property and it was converted into a school. In the early 1970's the Assemblies of God in Great Britain had bought the property and over the years developed it into a beautiful campus. We felt honored to lead this prestigious institution.

That is why the prospect of my life being interrupted by a dream was not an attractive one. I loved what we were doing and the privilege that was ours to lead a ministry training institution with students scattered literally around the world.

It was our practice to eat lunch in the College cafeteria and then retire to our beautiful little home hidden behind mature hedges on the extremity of the campus. Of course, this brief daily interlude had to include tea. Everything is tolerable with a good cup of tea!

Carol was desperate to articulate the dream. It had not left her throughout the day and was as vivid now as when she had actually dreamt it. She had concluded that I was not going to be sympathetic to her off loading the dream on me. With a cup of tea in her hand she leaned her head back on the sofa and passionately asked God what was happening and why the dream was so vivid. Was this really a dream from God? Could this be more than simply a graphic dream similar to others that she had? In that instant she felt certain that she knew what God was saying to us. She knew in no uncertain terms that God was talking about our next assignment.

We loved what we had been called to do in the UK. The College that we had the privilege of leading had extended its influence around the world. Graduate programs were being offered on three continents. We were assisting a large university in the US with developing a PhD program and the campus was thriving with men and women preparing for Christian ministry. The African diaspora was establishing churches across the UK and many of their leaders were turning to us to help in their training. In every sense it was a rich and fulfilling time of our lives.

However, denominational leadership had changed and some of the early signs were somewhat ominous to me. As a rule, Pentecostal denominations have never forged an effective theology of vocation. This has resulted in an awkward relationship between Bible Colleges and other Pentecostal institutions of higher education and their denominational base. I will have more to say on this as this book draws to a close. In my heart I knew that there were strong headwinds coming my way and that the fulfilling days of leading the College were coming to an end.

That's where the dream began to make sense – at least in part. Many aspects of the first part of the dream seemed to describe our position exactly. We agreed that retelling this aspect of what Carol saw was not helpful, and so we have only shared it with a few trusted friends. But it really helped us. We felt God was leading us and preparing us. The dream helped us make some good decisions that stood us in good stead over the coming months.

Carol vividly remembers the ending of the first part of her dream. She felt like a theatre curtain was closing. (This also proved reassuring to us in the months to come.) Then the dream changed dramatically as another scene opened. We were sitting in a car with me in the driver's seat. Behind us was a river and Carol was urging me to drive forward. For some reason I seemed hesitant to put the car in gear and drive away. In retrospect, I know now that I really did not want to leave the happy place that we were in. Carol became more urgent and then looked behind her. On the back seat of the car was a baby and it lay motionless. She cried out and wept as she told me that the baby was dead. She said it again, "The baby is dead!"

Her motherly instinct caused her to reach back and touch the little, lifeless body. To her delight the baby stirred, and she immediately reached backwards to pick it up. "The baby is alive, is alive!" she said again and again. With unbridled joy she took the baby into her arms, began to nurture it and, in that ecstatic moment, she woke up from the dream. No wonder she was troubled. The dream was so clear, so vivid. She could not prevent herself from shaking my shoulder asking me to please to wake up.

Neither of us knew how to process the dream. Carol was so troubled by it that she found an opportunity to share it with three of our closest friends. They listened patiently but could offer no specific advice. After years of Christian leadership, we found ourselves in the unusual and awkward place of not knowing what to do with an experience that seemed to be so supernatural in so many ways. Carol buried the dream in her heart, and I decided to forget about it.

From time to time we wondered if the next assignment was back to our homeland of South Africa where many years before we had been actively involved in caring for children whose families and communities had been devastated by the HIV/AIDS epidemic. We did our best to keep alert and prayerful. We wanted more than anything, to be doing exactly what God wanted us to do.

It seemed promising when I received an invitation to travel to London to meet a prominent Christian leader. He was the global leader of a dynamic ministry that cared for orphans in Africa. We met in one of the beautiful and ornate tea rooms of the famous London store Selfridges. At first it seemed as though things might be making sense and that Carol's dream was proving to be God helping us find His will. The offer was a great one. Leadership of all the training programs in this sizeable ministry, international travel, global opportunities. I left the meeting grateful for the prospect of a wonderful and new open door.

We have always been committed to processing the call and nudges of God by consistently following a pattern. We discuss the prospect much and often. We pray. We listen carefully as we share our daily devotional. We often consult trusted friends. Applying these disciplines, we were soon convinced that this wonderful door was not the one for us to walk through.

And so began the emotional journey of saying farewell to our team in the UK and ending our tenure leading one of Europe's premier Bible colleges and graduate schools. The process was made even more intense by the knowledge that, for the first time in our lives, we were leaving to a completely unknown and uncertain future. We had always believed that you never leave *"from"* but rather leave *"to,"* but this time around that was not to be.

I recall the care and support of very special friends at this time. Our dearest friends Ken and Christiane Williamson were faithful, kind and generous. Ken has since passed away, but we will forever remember their love. Again and again, we have proved that friendship and relationships count much more than strategy and planning. This was even more the case as we packed a container, moved out of our lovely home in the English countryside and embarked on an unknown and uncertain future.

Throughout the years that we had served in the UK, we had maintained a small home in North Carolina. Our children, Anna and Jay had been able to make good use of it. After Anna married Rich, they were able to use the house for a year as they planned and built a house of their own. We were so grateful to be able to support them in this way. Likewise, Jay stayed at the home for several years during this period. It seemed natural that we should return to this quiet and safe place in order to discover the plans that God had for us going forward. Carol has always had the most profound faith. She was not distressed at all and reveled in being closer to family. I am not given to anxiety, but I do feel the responsibility of providing for my family keenly at times. We now found ourselves in a very vulnerable place.

We did what we knew best. We kept the faith, spoke much to each other and felt reassured that God was in full control. Years of the faithfulness of a loving God now proved to be very reassuring. Our days were happy and full. But there was still no clear direction about what should be filling our lives.

Well over three decades of Christian service convinced us that God had a plan for what we were hoping would be the most fruitful years of our ministry. We took time to pray. As always, we kept in close touch with friends. We kept alert. What followed did not seem in line with anything that we had experienced. The dream, the exit from the UK and the uncertainty of a new season in the US did not prepare us for the following month or two.

Before giving details on what was about to occur, I must create some context. Over several years both Carol and I had a growing sense that we would be serving God in some capacity in the US. As Christian leaders we had observed the secularization of Europe. While secularization is not something that Christians should fear, the subtle undermining of religious freedom which secularized politicians and bureaucrats impose was startling to us. We had closely observed the rampant secular agenda in Europe and were noticing that by the early 2000's America was also rapidly secularizing. Eroding religious freedoms, conflicting moral values and the imposition of policies that were certain to create conflict for Christian institutions were becoming more and more evident to us. Some years before, Carol had completed a cutting-edge PhD project in which she examined in great depth the response of Christian leaders in the UK as they faced the secular agenda. Authority structures had changed. Moral ambiguity was everywhere present. Culture shift was obvious. As she examined these factors it was evident to her, through careful empirical study, that Christian leaders were largely not handling this cultural change well. And now we saw similar patterns across the United States. In fact, every time we flew in from across the Atlantic it was increasingly more evident. We became convinced that we were to somehow play a constructive role in helping Christian leaders in the US manage the culture wars.

Now we were back in the US, our adopted land. We had no doubt that God was completely in control. We loved being nearer family. We experienced the benefit of friendships that we had carefully maintained over many years. Making and keeping friends has always been important to us. Almost daily I deliberately engage with friends near and far. I never get tired of sustaining the gift of friendship. We now found ourselves on the receiving end of great friendships.

As we arrived back in the US one of these dear friends asked us to spend a weekend with his church's youth leaders at a delightful retreat center near Chicago. We were amazed at the hospitality and generosity that they lavished on us. In fact, on the last night we discovered that we had been booked into a lovely hotel in downtown Chicago. We walked the Golden Mile, enjoyed some gourmet coffee and even explored a high-end department store. As we made our way through one of the departments, we found an almost unbelievable sale on the most beautiful set of dinner ware. We had always hoped that we might own a set like this one day. The sale got better and better. Free extras, no cost for shipping and then a final 15% off at the end. They virtually gave us the set! Of course, we bought it. We felt spoiled, loved and appreciated. The whole experience was cathartic and spoke to us of the faithfulness of a faithful God.

Other long-term friends reached out to us. Multiple opportunities began to present themselves, and there was a growing certainty that we were not to wander in uncertain vulnerability. Our faithful God was crafting a perfect plan for the next phase of our lives. One of these friends had first met us more than thirty years before on a visit to the college we were leading in South Africa. He was now the missionary-in-residence at a college in the vast northern plains in faraway North Dakota.

One conversation led to another and by the winter of 2011 we had an invitation extended to us to conduct a spiritual emphasis series of services and consultations at Trinity Bible College in Ellendale, North Dakota. A careful search of the map revealed that the College was situated in a very small town just five miles north of the South Dakota state line in the southeast part of the state. It seemed an unlikely place for a Bible college and even more unlikely place for us to want to visit – especially during the winter months. Even a mention of the words "North Dakota" would raise people's eyebrows. Most were quite verbal in their perceptions of how far away this place was and, more importantly, how cold it gets in North Dakota.

However, our friends were insistent, and so we made arrangements to continue a ministry trip to the Midwest by driving further west to Ellendale. It was January 2012. As we drove the long miles across the flat landscape of the northern plains, I understood how people could believe in a flat earth. Although we have come to love the plains, on a cold, misty day in January there is not much to enjoy in terms of scenery. Everything is bleak and grey. Huge grain elevators break the landscape, and every now and again there is a row of trees standing dismally in the mist. Most of the small towns have no more than a gas station and maybe a drab fast-food outlet. This journey was not encouraging us.

We stopped in the South Dakota town of Aberdeen. Our journey had already seemed endless, and we still had nearly an hour to go. After filling the tank with gas, we made our way through the mist to highway 281 and the forty-mile journey due north. You can get almost anywhere in the northern plains with just a left and a right turn. Roads are all on a grid pattern and only go either north and south or east and west. Every now and again there are gentle bends that I am told help compensate for the earth's curvature and ensure that a due north trajectory is maintained.

Eventually we reached the stop sign at the corner of Highway 281 and Main Street, Ellendale. It is unimpressive. No traffic light, no signs. We turned eastward and made our way through the small town. We noticed that there was an "akery" right on Main Street. It caught our attention until we realized that it was actually the bakery and that the "B" had fallen off the sign. Sadly, the bakery shut down a few years later. Where had we come to?

As you exit the built-up part of the little town of Ellendale and drive a few blocks further east the majestic pillars of Davidson Hall emerge, and it becomes clear that there is a substantial collection of buildings ahead. I will never forget seeing those pillars for the first time. They would become the center of another story which you will need to read about later in this book. I do recall that my heart leapt inside me, a feeling I could not reconcile with all my other senses at the time.

Carol's dream seemed a long time ago and was far from our thoughts as we made our way onto the campus of Trinity Bible College. There were rumors that the College was not in a good place financially and its viability was being questioned. However, we were given a warm welcome, enjoyed reuniting with our friends and looked forward to a productive time with what was obviously not an insignificant group of students.

The next day our first commitment was in the chapel. It felt a little old fashioned to us. We sat awkwardly on the platform along with college administrators. At first there was not much that commended itself to us. Carol leaned over to me and whispered in my ear, "These students seem dead!" We had come from an extraordinarily vibrant college environment, and, at the time, this place did not compare. I was hesitant as I stood to preach that first time. I knew that people from the northern plains with their German and Scandinavian heritage had a reputation for being stoic and unemotive. In fact, everything that I had been told seemed to be true of this chapel service. There was not much of an outward response to my preaching initially. I pushed through and even felt compelled to extend an invitation for a tangible response. I asked those challenged by what I had shared to stand. To my amazement the majority quickly responded and willingly stood to their feet.

Some spontaneously made their way to the front of the chapel and stood with expectancy asking God to do a work in their lives. It was most encouraging. In fact, Carol commented as we left the chapel that the students were not as dead as she had initially thought.

That first day passed in a happy way with good conversations. We met someone whom we had known for years by his good reputation. After making several visits to the beautiful Bible College called "Monte Esperanza" in Portugal we had heard many times of the indefatigable Sam Johnson. And now he was here in this far away town. We had heard that he was somehow involved in this College, but we did not know how. His enthusiasm was unbounded! It was not long before he was showing us around. It was cold. We will never forget. It was January 19, and it was 19 degrees below zero. Within minutes of walking across the campus it felt like we had lost our legs. We were not adequately dressed, but Sam insisted that we should see the whole place. We walked across to the abandoned old President's House. (This is another story that I will tell later in the book). By this time, we were becoming increasingly aware that there were those who were hoping that our visit to Ellendale would result in more than a few days of services.

Carol preached in chapel the next day. Once again, the response was enthusiastic. These were quality young men and women. We were definitely warming to the place. Unbeknown to us, a group of the Executive Committee of the Board of Trustees had joined us on the campus.

The Conference Room down the corridor of the Student Life Center is unremarkable in almost every way. Its ventilation is not good, it has no natural light and lacked atmosphere of any kind. But that is where we were told there would be a meeting, and it would be greatly appreciated if we would be willing to attend. It was late morning, and the atmosphere was awkward. Why were we there? More importantly, why had a committee of the Board convened at that exact time? It was clear that a plot was being hatched!

I tried to break the ice with some general conversation. We

still did not seem to be getting to the reason for the meeting. I remember thinking that we would be gone in little over 24 hours. This meeting could never have any significance. And so, with a degree of cheek and wit, I suggested that someone ask us what we were planning to do with the rest of our lives. Someone did! I managed to answer with some generalities - all completely non-committal of course.

Do you remember Carol's dream? The car, the baby, the nurturing, the sudden awakening. It was the furthest thought from our minds until the Chair of the Board of Trustees spoke up. Stephen Schaible is the District Superintendent of the South Dakota District of the Assemblies of God. He and Rachel have become the dearest of friends, but I did not know him at all. I did know that he and a mutual friend of ours loved hunting. They would often go out for a day shooting little prairie dogs. The ranchers appreciated them for doing this, but I had never been a hunter and this was an introduction to something that I learned was an important part of peoples' lives in this part of the country. So, I did know that he was something of an outdoorsman. When he began to speak, his choice of words seemed decidedly uncharacteristic.

He informed us that there had been some serious discussions about the viability of Trinity Bible College and whether it would perhaps be more expedient to take steps to close it. The others in the room seemed to be in agreement. Then he used a metaphor that immediately galvanized my and Carol's attention. He stated that they had wondered if the "baby had died." What a strange metaphor. It seemed so out of character. Why use this image? But we immediately recognized the phrase. Carol's dream flashed before our eyes. That was the exact phrase that had been used by Carol in her dream. She had said repeatedly through tears, "The baby is dead! The baby is dead!" I braced myself and the following words Superintendent Schaible used drove home that something remarkable was transpiring. He stated that there had been a consensus that if someone would "pick the baby up and nurture it there was still life and hope." I have no idea what my face was saying, but I did my best not to give away that my heart was tumbling around inside me. I instinctively knew that God was orchestrating something beyond what we could imagine at the time.

The meeting concluded, and Carol and I escaped to our hotel room. We said little to each other. We had lived long enough and loved each other deeply enough to be quietly submissive to what we were perceiving was the will of God for our lives. At the meal with our friends that evening we said nothing. We were determined to give nothing away. Perhaps there was a lingering hope that our future assignment might be in a place that did not feel so remote, or a ministry that was not so vulnerable.

The next morning, we met early in the President's office. As we made our way into the office Sam Johnson slid off his chair and onto his knees. Looking up at us with clasped hands he pleaded with us to come. The President at the time remarked that he would resign within an hour of us expressing our willingness to accept the invitation. I begged Sam to get off his knees but realized that this was more than theatrics. He had already invested so much into the future of the College and clearly believed that it was potentially a bright one. Again, he pleaded. We assured him that we would give it serious consideration.

We left later that day. It was still ice cold. It was misty and dreary, but the chemistry of our hearts had changed. We felt strangely at peace. We quietly absorbed the reassurances of a faithful God who was still leading us, still committed to us and still planning to use us fruitfully.

How grateful I was to have a wife by my side who desired the will of God as fervently as I ever could. By the time a few hours had passed in the car we smiled gently at each other and knew that the next assignment for our lives was settled. In fact, as we drove into the next substantial town, Carol insisted that we should stop at the mall. She walked deliberately to the store that had winter coats. I tried to dissuade her. I told her that even if we did go to Trinity, it would not be until the summer. She was determined. She found a coat, tried it on and declared that this represented her earnest that she would gladly submit to God's will, and that we would be moving to the northern plains. We were going to commit to leading Trinity Bible College.

Aerial View Trinity Bible College

We had no idea what awaited us.

CHAPTER TWO

The Die is Cast

It was the most beautiful early winter day in Johannesburg, South Africa. Built at a high point on Africa's continental plateau the "City of Gold" started as a small mining camp in the late 1880's. It burgeoned into a significant metropolis and when I was born in the 1950's, it was a bustling, sophisticated city.

Winters can be quite cold in Johannesburg because of its altitude, but normally the frost thaws and the comforting warmth of winter sunshine takes the chill off the air. It was a morning like this that found me sitting at my desk in an annex to the well-established church known as Fairview Assembly of God. At the tender age of only 25 I was the senior pastor of this great mother church. We were enjoying a good season. The church was growing, new young people were filling the pews and I was reveling in the opportunity to use my preaching gift on a weekly basis.

But this morning was different. My happy circumstances and my heart seemed to be out of sync. I had so much to be grateful for. I had recently completed my tour of duty as an army chaplain with many months serving in the midst of the horrible Angolan Bush War. Carol was never certain as to whether I would come home in a plane or a body bag. Our two little children were now in such a secure place. We had moved to a home just a few houses away from Carol's childhood home. We had already planned the schools our children would attend, and we were appreciated as the young pastors of a dynamic church. Still this morning was different.

I hardly felt like praying. At that moment I was not sure if God would hear me. My soul seemed strangely ill at ease. I am not even sure how I discerned my mood. I knew I did not like what I felt. Life had come at Carol and me hard and fast for the previous number of years. We had returned to South Africa from pastoring a church in England. We had two babies under the age of two years old. We had come through the separation of my army service which was required by conscription at the time. We were now senior pastoring a well-known church. Perhaps it was all a bit too much. And yet that is not how I felt.

I remember groaning inwardly. And then it happened. Whether it was a tangible or spiritual experience I do not know. It was as real as anything I had ever experienced. My study flamed with light. I can still remember a glow along the bookcase to my right-hand side. I instinctively knew that this was good. I knew it was God. It was not unsettling; it was comforting and real. Then, immediately I knew three things without even a hint of doubt.

I knew in that moment that we were to leave pastoral ministry; we were going to impact nations and that we were called to trust on behalf of others. The first two made sense but I could not understand what the latter meant. Now, years later I understand what God was calling us to, but at the time it was a mystery. I still know, because I know, because I know that the experience I had that early winter day was a real one. It has defined our lives. The die was cast.

I ran downstairs, through the wrought iron gate at the side of the church building and drove home as fast as I could. Our home was an older ranch style house with mature pine trees along the driveway. I brought the car to a jolting stop, opened the door and ran along the path to the front door. I hardly paused as I pushed it open and burst into the living room. Carol was obviously startled.

Giving no explanation I reached out, grabbed her hand and literally dragged her down the passage. I pinned her up against the bedroom wall and breathlessly announced to her that I confidently knew that God was moving us into a new dimension of ministry.

I have said this thousands of times throughout our marriage, but I really did marry the most remarkable girl. Her willingness to serve God, to trust my sense of His leading and to be a part of any adventure He might bring our way has never ceased to amaze me. Despite the upheaval of the previous couple of years, the happy thoughts of raising our kids in a secure environment and her happiness at being in a familiar place, she quickly encouraged my newfound enthusiasm. She affirmed what I was feeling. She assured me of her desire to also find God's best for our lives. We felt ecstatic. God was at work and every spiritual instinct inside us was confirming this.

By the end of that week, I began to doubt the experience that had so rapidly invaded my life. I desperately wanted to hold on to the ecstasy, the promise, the hope. But routine started to settle in. Carol and I agreed that what we needed was to be purposefully self-disruptive, and so we made up our minds to travel about four hours east of where we lived at the time to visit some dear friends. They were working at a Christian guest farm and had a home big enough to welcome us. We put the children in the car and left about midday on the Friday.

Driving east from Johannesburg you pass the towns that were made rich by gold mining. Huge mountains of waste material from the mines dot the landscape. It is busy and noisy. After a short time with nothing remarkable about the landscape, the mine dumps give way to smoke-belching power stations as you drive into the coal mining center of the country. Huge open cast mines scar the landscape. For anyone with even a hint of an awareness of creation care, the scene is jarring. In winter an atmospheric inversion ensures that the smoke hangs low. Thankfully, the road leads further eastwards and after a while you become aware that you are descending. The continental plateau gives way rapidly to the ragged edges of an ancient geological upheaval. This is the southern extreme of the great rift valley that divides parts of east Africa. It is a land of great beauty and wonder. The vegetation thickens and quite suddenly becomes sub-tropical. It is not unusual to see a troop of baboons keeping busy just off to the side of the road. The air thickens and the dry high-altitude air gives way to more humid air.

We took this road that Friday afternoon and arrived at our friends' home in the late afternoon. The tropical fruit trees that filled their lush garden seemed to join together in welcoming us and we felt grateful for the opportunity. We were also expectant. We wanted God to keep speaking into our lives and we were doing all we could to remain attentive and responsive.

By the next day the only spiritual experience that we felt we could record was a brief moment the night before. Carol had remarked that she had felt that the words of the prophet Isaiah were relevant to our situation. "As high as the heavens are above the earth so are my ways above yours." The words were reassuring but did not seem to help as we prayed earnestly for God to reveal what our next calling was going to be. It was with a sense of disappointed resignation that we began the four-hour journey home. We were no nearer discerning our future than we had been the day before.

The quiet drone of the car engine put both children to sleep. It was quiet as we began the ascent back to the noise and smoke of the industrial belt east of Johannesburg. Although different in many ways, I became conscious of the same sense of God's presence as I had felt earlier in the week in my church study. God was present – quiet, reassuring, leading. Thoughts began to race through my mind. Although I could trace precursors to these thoughts as I reflected later, they seemed to come from nowhere. My heart leapt, my mind was alert and I sensed God speaking very directly to me. In fact, I felt so certain of the experience that I turned to Carol and confidently told her that I knew what God wanted to tell us.

I said it would be called "Africa School of Missions," and that we would send people all over the earth. I could hardly get the words out fast enough. We would train people and motivate them to be missionaries. We would mobilize churches. The dream language flowed as I allowed my sense of God's will for our lives to tumble out of my mouth. Again, I found a willing accomplice in Carol. She affirmed what I was saying. It was so real, and yet, was already taking us way beyond what we could comprehend. The sense of God's leading was so profound that by the time the journey was over, the car unpacked, and we were back in the quiet of our home I took out a writing pad and, as fast as I could write, recorded all that I felt God had said. It ran to six pages. Training, serving, mobilizing and reaching lost people were concepts that filled that primitive document.

For the first time in South Africa

A full time residential charismatic Bible training course with special emphasis on WORLD MISSIONS

Beautiful campus in lovely Eastern Transvaal
Excellent facilities
Full Theological Diploma
Cross cultural exposure and ministry
Pre-field mission training and orientation

Courses offered
1. One year Christian Worker's Certificate.
2. Two year Theological Diploma.
3. Specialist Missions Training.
4. Completion of all the above leads to a Licentiate in Christian Ministries.

AFRICA SCHOOL OF MISSIONS

Applications and registrations for January 1985 now received.
For prospectus and information write to:
THE REGISTRAR, P.O. BOX 530, BEDFORDVIEW 2008.

Amazingly, this document was foundational to all that we were about to do, and every part of it became a reality. But we were a long way away from that being accomplished. Young and eager as we were, we decided that the best thing to do was to trust God for a property of some sort. I was deeply impressed by the stories that Lauren Cunningham had recorded regarding the work of Youth With A Mission. If God could do it for him, why not for me?

Within a week or two we had the kids in the car again. Past the mine dumps, past the smoke-belching power stations, down the African escarpment and back to our friends' farm. The nearest town was called Nelspruit. It was a beautiful little town nestled among hills and surrounded on virtually every side by citrus orchards. When the orange trees come into blossom the scent hangs heavily in the air. It is hard to describe the beauty and the amazing aroma. Quickly the small green oranges form and then they burst into a colorful carpet of rich orbs against the verdant green leaves. Everything about the area was beautiful and we felt certain this was where God wanted us.

I knew absolutely nothing about missionary training. Perhaps it was this naivety that God most valued about us at the time. We walked boldly into the office of a local real estate agent. For some reason I carried a brief case with me. There was almost nothing in it, but I assumed that it would help give the appearance of our ability to negotiate the purchase of a property.

We decided a farm would be best. Perhaps one with some barns that could be converted to dormitories. Our enthusiasm and vision knew no bounds. We visited the first farm. It had panoramic views. The farmhouse was substantial and in our minds we had already moved in. We thought the large living room would make a great lecture hall. We actually paced the ground believing God would give it to us.

Later that day we visited another farm. It was even better! This one had a series of outbuildings that would easily convert into accommodation. We were ecstatic. Imagine enthusiastic young people entrusting us with their lives and relocating to this beautiful place for a year or two. There were vast areas of unplanned urban development within a few minutes' drive from these properties, and we knew that we could almost immediately develop mission outreaches into these areas. By the end of a couple of days we had walked over several farms, imagined hundreds of young people devoting their lives to missionary service, and found ourselves signing an offer to purchase the property we felt was best suited to the developing vision that we had.

It hardly occurred to us that we had no money. We had no doubt whatsoever that God would provide. With a high level of audacity, I called a pastor friend and suggested that the best thing he could do was to have their large church lend us all that we needed. He graciously declined. This surprised me but I continued undaunted. That was until the real estate agent called to say that our offer for the farm had been rejected.

We were astounded. That kind of thing does not happen in the all the faith-filled stories in the books that we were reading. We were convinced that the farmer who had so curiously rejected our offer would have multiple bad harvests, for God would certainly not bless him!

The sense of faith and confidence that had developed over the past several weeks melted away. Disappointment quicky replaced our sense of optimism. Doubt set in. It was a crippling feeling with so many unanswered questions. Had the powerful experiences just been the illusions of a young and enthusiastic mind? Had the efforts to discover the transcendent, the ethereal will of God all been a silly game?

I do remember with great clarity the way in which I expressed myself in prayer. With resignation I let God know that if all these experiences had really been of Him then I was content to let it wait whether it was for one week, one month, one year or more. It was a mixed emotion at best. I was not going to lose faith but, at the same time, the reserves of optimistic, action-filled faith were all used up.

Our family quickly got back into routine. Longer-term plans began to be revisited in our thinking and conversation. Our commitment to the local church we were leading remained steadfast. But we could not help but reflect on the ecstatic, faith-filled experiences of the previous weeks.

God understood my temperament so well. It only took a matter of ten days. Although we can trace the ways in which what was to transpire took place, in the moment it seemed like the phone call that I received came from nowhere. A nice sounding gentleman called me and, in his opening comments, told me that he had heard that I "had a vision." I was amazed at how quickly the spark of vision and passion returned. I assured him that I certainly did and proceeded to fill in the developing details. Concepts about training, sending and serving tumbled out of my heart. He listened carefully and asked if we could meet in the near future.

I let Carol know about the unexpected phone call and she quickly suggested that we invite our new friend for dinner. We agreed on a date and it was arranged. We waited in keen expectation. What was transpiring?

Carol has always been a great hostess. Guests are welcomed to a freshly cleaned home. Careful thought has gone into the meal. There is almost always a starter of some kind. Meals have been central to our lives in leadership. Almost nothing has given us as much pleasure as inviting guests into our home. Carol carefully and creatively sets the table. Where possible, there is a display of fresh flowers. She always amazes me with her creative touch.

Then there is the meal. Normally a roast of either chicken or beef is sending out its rich aroma from the kitchen as our guests enter the house. Our new friend was to be treated to a roast chicken dinner with all the trimmings. However, he did not come at the time arranged. An hour went by as the chicken dried out in the oven. Frustration set in as we watched another fifteen minutes tick by.

Eventually Gerry Schoonbee arrived. We knew by this time

that he was an influential businessman, but that was about all. Carol was obviously frustrated by his late arrival, and it did not help things when he said little about it except a passing apology. He made some enquiries about what I had been sensing God was saying to me. Despite the dinner being served an hour or more late, Gerry seemed to relish every mouthful and soon announced his gratitude and headed for his car. I could not believe it. Were we not supposed to talk through some of the exciting details of my vision? Was he not going to say why he was interested in the first place? He left and I stood looking somewhat forlorn as I watched his expensive car turn the corner. He was gone. I knew his name but that was about all. I had no idea what his phone number was or how we could keep in touch.

Again, routine set in. Managing the day-to-day responsibilities of leading a growing church and an internal chemistry that suggested there was another task at hand was not easy for a twenty-eight-year-old. Eventually I received a call from Gerry. He informed me that he wanted us to meet his wife, Mary. When I told Carol, she quickly informed me that there was not going to be a dinner involved this time.

They arrived at our home with their very young granddaughter in tow. I could tell instantly that Mary was a Scot. Her rich accent reminded me of my own Scottish grandmother. It was strangely comforting until I realized that she was about to interrogate Carol and me about our vision. Unlike the meal some weeks before the questions kept coming. They wanted detail that I could not give. Remember, all I had was six handwritten sheets of paper and a passionate heart. I did produce those notes and was grateful that I had taken the time to write down what I had felt God had told me. Two hours flew by. Thanking us for our time Gerry and Mary and their little one got into their car and left. Again, I remember distinctly feeling that I had no idea what was going on. Who were these people? Where was this going? It was not going to take long for us to understand it all.

We began to discover what remarkable people Gerry and Mary Schoonbee were. Gerry had become extremely successful as the Chief Executive Officer of one of Africa's largest construction companies. Mary was a nurse by background, a Roman Catholic by upbringing and an amazing homemaker. Their home was furnished with valuable antiques. Their children had all attended Catholic schools and Gerry, though raised as a Dutch Reformed member had concentrated on his business interests. Early into his fiftieth year of life someone had extended Gerry an invitation to attend a businesspersons' breakfast. Thinking himself to be mildly religious, he agreed to attend. It was there that he was confronted with the amazing and gracious love of Jesus for him. He spontaneously responded and, in that moment, became a totally committed follower of Christ.

The transformation in his life was so obvious that it was not long before Mary was demanding answers. What had happened to Gerry? Early in their marriage they had agreed that they would never speak of religion or politics. They were both strong willed people and believed that this agreement would ensure their compatibility. So now Gerry was in a quandary. He had agreed not to talk on the subject of religion. Mary was insistent, and as Gerry shared about the transforming power of Christ and how he had committed his life to Jesus, Mary felt her heart warmed. Gerry was articulating everything that she had longed for most of her life. She soon became an equally committed Christ follower.

Their newfound faith caused Gerry and Mary to become radically committed in many ways. Most tangibly was a desire to be generous with their bountiful wealth. Through an equally committed business associate, the Schoonbees had become involved in several mission projects near the beautiful town of White River, just up the road from Nelspruit. It was exactly where we had walked over so many farms. They soon invited us to join them there.

We arrived at the Good News Center outside of White River in early October of 1984. It was hard to imagine a more beautiful location. The Center was a complex of buildings that had been a successful resort until the Schoonbees had bought it and spent much time and resources on converting it into a conference center that would cater largely for Christian groups. Set on over fifty acres of land, the property slopes gently into a shallow valley through which the Small Sand River flows. A dam had been built in the corner of the property, and so now there was a lovely lake, often inhabited by several large hippopotami. Standing on the balcony in front of the spacious cafeteria the majestic granite dome of Legogote Mountain rises into the sky ahead of you. Verdant indigenous bush clings to its side and the whole view is majestic. The only interruption to the silence and the beauty is a noisy troop of vervet monkeys scurrying by. If you walk to the highest point of the property, it is possible to see across into the vast expanse of the Kruger National Park.

Although it was the end of a dry winter when we first arrived, the place filled us with awe. The entrance into the main building had a soaring ceiling lined with local pine wood. Bedrooms were built in rows of two or four throughout the lush sub-tropical gardens. The swimming pool and nearly new tennis courts looked stunning in this setting.

We were ushered into the large lounge. A beautiful stone fireplace filled one wall. Furnishings were tasteful and it was obvious that there had been a considerable amount of refurbishment taking place. The obligatory tray of tea was brought in and set before us. Carol quickly volunteered to pour the tea, and we waited eagerly to see why we had been invited to this beautiful place. Mary and Gerry proceeded to tell us that they had confidence in our vision. They believed that we could train people and that missionary people could influence many nations. We were humbled by their confidence in a young and inexperienced couple.

I recall the moment like it was yesterday. With beautiful vistas outside the floor to ceiling windows, a warm cup of tea in our hands and the reassuring voices of our new friends, Carol and I were told that God had spoken to Mary and Gerry. In fact, they were so certain that they had heard from God that they proceeded to inform that everything we saw – from the tennis courts in the expansive gardens to the teaspoons in the well-equipped kitchen was ours to do what God had called us to do. They were not leasing or loaning the place. They were donating it and would make sure that the title to the property was transferred at their own expense. Within months they were completely true to their word.

What a moment. We were overwhelmed by it all. It felt like we glided through the place almost in a trance. The next morning, we rose and knew it was all real. Africa School of Mission had been born. We quickly set about planning our move to White River. A small faculty was recruited. I traveled the length and breadth of the country recruiting our first intrepid group of students. Rooms were prepared, cafeteria staff bought in supplies, and in January 1985, classes began.

The adventure of the next ten years is the subject of a book on its own. Our response to the Mozambican refugee crisis, the launch of a primary health care program, the commissioning of brave young missionaries and graduates serving in more than forty different nations filled our lives. Building after building was erected all as a result of generous friends standing with us. A library, dedicated in memory of my parents, was established and grew to be one of the best theological collections in southern Africa.

For Carol and me the die was cast. Somehow, we knew that whatever else we did, the training and educating of men and women for God's work would be the major focus. Our lives would never be the same again.

Ten years later we left the work we had begun. A great church in Queensland, Australia, invited us to lead the church, but also to help establish a ministry training college in southeast Queensland. Seven happy years were to follow.

During this time, I felt a growing sense of spiritual concern for churches in Europe. By early 1990, our lives took another turn and we committed to a missionary training and mobilizing ministry across the European continent. This led to our Alma Mater recruiting me to be their President.

And so, we moved to the United Kingdom. Mattersey Hall was the largest Pentecostal college in Europe and the next eight years of our lives were filled with the delight of training hundreds of key leaders. We had the very special joy of bringing much innovation to the Graduate School at Mattersey and the years passed with much fulfillment and joy.

I had never taken time to process the call to Christian higher education. It was as though this call had found me. Our lives had been shaped around training and educating people for God's work. Then, came the dream.

CHAPTER THREE

A Rich Heritage

The sun sets slowly in the northern plains during summer. It seems to linger on the horizon filling the sky with a blaze of colors worthy of the boldest artist's pallet. It is an austere beauty. No mountains to break the view, vast vistas invade the senses, and it is difficult not to be in wonder.

This is North Dakota. It is beautiful, brutal, and outstanding in so many ways. After the long evenings of summer, the fall blows in and temperatures plummet. It is not uncommon for weeks or even months to pass with subzero temperatures. Lakes and rivers freeze, the wind howls and the days are short. And yet it is in this land of extremes that a large proportion of America's food is grown. Out of a dozen or more staple crops, North Dakota is the leading producer of at least seven or eight. Most of the wheat that produces the pasta we eat is grown on these fertile plains.

Farmers' fields dip below the horizon, they are so vast. North Dakota suffered the ravages of the "Dust Bowl" drought of the thirties, but quickly recovered. Now huge tractors pull the biggest plows in the world and produce mountains of corn and soybeans, sunflowers, and alfalfa. Thousands of cattle graze the low hills and the dry grass pastures produce some of the best beef in the world. What an amazing part of the country.

If this bounty was not enough, the Bakken oil fields of northwest North Dakota quietly and unassumingly produce energy in an efficient and relatively environmentally safe way. Humble ranchers and farmers have been made wealthy beyond their dreams, but their old trucks, plain clothes and modest homes give no clue to their financial resources.

It is in this paradoxical land of beauty and cold, bleakness and bounty that some of the hardiest and most gracious people on earth have made their home. With stoic Scandinavian and German ancestors, they settled the land with one-roomed homesteads. They educated their children in small rural schools, and they subdued the land to make it some of the most productive real estate on the planet.

It is not a surprise then, that some of these strong-willed people decided that their churches should be served by young people who shared their values and understood the unique way of life they had adopted. A training college that allowed students to fit in with the agrarian calendar, be home for harvest and then serve local churches with courage and resilience was what was needed. And thus, in 1948 regional church leaders, modestly dressed, but relatively affluent, farmers and local businesspeople decided to establish a Bible college.

The North Dakotan Assemblies of God Fellowship already owned a campsite along the banks of Devils Lake in the north of the state. It was sparse and had no grand buildings, no library and simple accommodation that was really designed to be used more in the summer than in the very cold winter months. Lakewood Park Bible Institute was established using these premises and immediately attracted a group of intrepid students, and a small faculty began to teach them.

Lakewood Bible Park Institute

Graduates began to plant churches, and soon most Assembly of God churches in the Dakotas were pastored by those who had graduated from Lakewood Park. Growth necessitated a move to Aberdeen, South Dakota, and not long after that a large former hospital in Jamestown, North Dakota was acquired for the growing school. It was called "Trinity" and the name was adopted. Trinity Bible College was established and was busily fulfilling its mission of training men and women for ministry in the Dakotas and beyond.

In the late 1960's and early 1970's the President at the time, Dr. Roy Wead, heard of the Ellendale campus of the University of North Dakota. It became known that the university was divesting itself of the expansive property, and Roy Wead used all his influence to secure the property. His son Doug wrote to me some years ago. As far as I know, what he wrote has never been recorded even though Doug published an outstanding book recording much of the history of the College around this time. As interest in the property ramped up, the competition as to who would acquire it was intense. This is what Wead informed me of:

The co-founder of Hewlett-Packard and former Secretary of Defense under Richard Nixon, David Packard, was leading a group of New York investors interested in bidding for the place.

Junior Achievement had proposed moving their New York headquarters to the Ellendale campus.

Renowned writer and Academy Award winner, Bud Schulberg, proposed that the campus be turned into a national writers' retreat. (Schulberg wrote the screenplay for the Marlon Brando classic, *On the Waterfront)*.

The National Police Officers Association of Venice, Florida proposed turning the campus into a specialized police academy.

Four different Native American tribes were making claims to the land, and their work was moving through the court system.

More than 40 different colleges and universities offered to buy the campus outright. For example, Northwestern University in Evanston, Illinois, proposed a campus extension in North Dakota.

There were dozens of foundations representing the mentally disabled who wanted to purchase the property for a specialized school.

There were more than a thousand bids and proposals, each with lawyers and thousands of pages of paperwork competing for the campus.

Roy Wead's tenacity kept strong through this extended time. Eventually, not only did his proposal succeed, but it was also transacted for a single dollar! Imagine, this not only required passage in the North Dakota House and a signature from the Governor. It also required an amendment to the North Dakota State constitution and, if that were not enough, it required a statewide vote. Decades have passed since these interesting days, but we can only imagine the infighting that took place.

Some years ago, I took a stroll on a warm summer's afternoon to the edge of our little town and wandered through the cemetery. Like so many towns in the Dakotas there is a Protestant cemetery and a Catholic one. I came across an unassuming grave with a small headstone. It was that of Roy Wead. I stood quietly as I recalled the personal sacrifice this brave man had made in securing a substantial university campus for a Bible College. It gave me pause as it related to my own term as President. Would I build and leave a legacy?

It was not all good news, however. Enough time has passed for the record to show that, despite the new facilities, the more than 20-year record of good work and the tenacious leadership of a godly President, to recall the denominational battle that ensued. The delicate balance of AG schools established on a regional basis was affected and there were many efforts to exclude Trinity Bible College from the AG fold. For example, Trinity was not permitted to advertise in the Pentecostal Evangel. According to Doug Wead, and I must concur, if Roy Wead had not been a member of the Executive Presbytery at the time and afforded the opportunity of passionate advocacy on behalf of Trinity, the College might well not have survived. These events have passed into history but add a texture and a layer to the rich heritage that has now combined to allow the writing of this amazing current story of Trinity Bible College and Graduate School.

Groups of graduates began to radiate out into the region. The Dakotas, Montana, Wyoming and even the eastern side of Washington soon had graduates pastoring their churches. Multiple other States and towns had Trinity alumni faithfully serving. I have met some of these people although many had passed on before we arrived in North Dakota. Resilient, pragmatic, and tough would be words I use to describe them. They are seldom demonstrative but have a keen sense of integrity. Their faithful lives speak of a faithful God.

Each successive President played their part and made valuable contributions. Others are better suited to tell their story than me. Suffice it to honor these people and the many that served alongside them through the decades. Well-loved teachers are still spoken of, faithful cooks and facilities services managers are recalled, at times with a humorous story, but always with respect.

Almost everyone that you encounter who had any length of time studying at Trinity will quickly recall the times in chapel when God spoke to them. Some delight in taking me to the exact spot at the front of the chapel where they encountered the presence of God and felt His direction to one task or another.

I recall one chapel service. We had a missionary leader addressing us. His stories from Southeast Asia were enthralling. I remember thinking how privileged we all were to hear these passionate communicators and their rich stories. I noticed that from time to time our speaker would pause and seem to recall something in his memory. He quickly moved on and then it happened again. He said several times that he felt like he had been to Trinity before, but then quickly corrected himself to say that this was his first visit. But he was obviously recalling something. And then he realized what it was. For years he had worked with missionary colleagues. They had served amongst some of the most resistant people groups in the nation they had felt called to. Evidently, several missionary couples had given up serving among these people. They had a long history of violence, and missionary service among them had been hard and unfruitful. But this couple was different. They served year after year. When rejected they loved back. When persecuted they responded with grace and forgiveness.

Finally, the missionary found words to express what he was sensing. He told us that the reason he felt as though he had visited Trinity before was that what he sensed in that chapel was exactly what he felt when he was in the presence of this brave missionary couple that he knew. Then he joined the dots in his thinking. They were Trinity alumni. His knowledge and profound respect for them seemed to be echoed in the atmosphere and spirit of a Trinity chapel service. The moment was extraordinary! I remember fighting back the tears as I imagined more and more of these brave young people serving sacrificially around the world. This was our heritage; this was our rich history.

Again, the sense of awe and responsibility of leading an

institution with these stories written into its history flooded my consciousness. I had to believe that the faithfulness of God that had brought the institution this far would propel it into the future.

All that optimism and hope was going to be tried in the early years of the new millennium. A combination of multiple factors put the College and its leadership under immense strain. There was a transition in Presidential leadership, a major building program and a growing regulatory environment. The latter placed the College under increased scrutiny with both the accrediting bodies and auditors.

The axe fell in early 2012, when the combination of an unrealistic debt burden and several academic issues resulted in the College suffering a double blow. Firstly, a "going concern" clause was added to the audited accounts. This meant that the professionals who analyzed the College finances on an annual basis were not convinced that the College could operate for another year. The Board was required to show some evidence as to whether operations could continue. The second blow was administered by our accreditors. The regional accrediting agency determined to make Trinity an example, and the Board took advice to voluntarily withdraw from their accreditation. The national accrediting agency had no alternative but to serve a "show cause" on the school. This is about as bad as it gets in the world of accreditation. The College was compelled to show reasonable cause as to its likelihood of being able to deliver the academic program it offered as presented in its catalogue.

These actions were ominous. One alone was enough to force action and close the school. Perhaps it was the rich heritage that somehow kept a small glow of hope alive. More likely it was the gentle urging of a faithful God that prevented a decision to close the College.

This was the situation we found when we arrived in Ellendale and assumed the leadership of the College. Notices for cutting off of water and electricity were issued, and in my first week in office

I had a nice gentleman come to visit me and proceed to tell me that there was no propane left in any of the tanks on our campus. With the winters that North Dakota has this was not good news at all. Debt was crippling and morale was low. But we had responded in a sense of great obedience to God, and now we needed some miracles in order to survive.

CHAPTER FOUR

Early Glimmers of Hope

The summer months in the northern plains are frenetic times. Farmers have a shorter growing season than in many other parts of the country. As soon as the ground has gone through a thaw those huge plows and planters rush up and down huge fields planting their valuable seed. Calves are born and dot the landscape with cuteness.

It is also a time when bugs, frogs, snakes, and insects of every kind emerge to reproduce in large numbers before the cold of winter blows in. They are everywhere. Every year it appears as though a plague of biblical proportions hits these little towns. In the years when the frogs proliferate the only good news is that they keep the clouds of mosquitoes in control. Driving down any roadway, the unavoidable and terrible sound of hundreds of frogs popping beneath the wheel of your vehicle is an unpleasant reminder that summer is here. Unbelievably, these cold plains also produce snakes. They emerge and slither through the grass eating box elder bugs in large numbers. It is difficult to choose what is best. Snakes or bugs? Frogs or mosquitoes? The long, warm evenings compensate for any discomfort that the vast number of unwanted creatures might produce.

It was in the middle of such a summer in 2012 that Carol and I drove across the country and arrived in Ellendale on a warm, late afternoon. Sitting in the driveway awaiting our arrival was a small welcome group. They had been assembled to help us move our few belongings into the small, prefabricated house that was to be our home for the next few years.

As the group rose from their little huddle on the driveway, I immediately recognized the 6-foot, 7-inch man who stood head and shoulders above the rest. This was Ian O'Brien. I had known Ian for several years, since he had been a student in a Graduate class that we were teaching in South Africa. Later he had graciously invited me to be the keynote speaker at the conference that he led in his church north of Cape Town. I was deeply impressed by the creativity and vitality that I experienced during that conference.

Ian O'Brien

We followed the adventures of Ian, his wife Heather, and their family. I was intrigued when I heard that they were relocating to the USA and even more amazed at the miraculous events surrounding their emigration. Then, they accepted the pastorate of a church in Virginia, and soon we were driving to see them and preach in Sunday services there. Again, the stature of this man both physically and intellectually could not help but leave an impression.

When I found out that Trinity Bible College had lost its Dean of Students just a few weeks before our anticipated arrival it seemed natural to me to enquire if Ian might be interested. To my delight he was, and before Carol and I could get to Ellendale, Ian and Heather along with their two boys and young daughter, not forgetting the two cats, had made the long trip from Virginia to North Dakota. And now he was welcoming us to our new home.

Little did I know how much of a significant role this couple would play in the years to come. As I write this, they have just accepted a pastoral position back in Virginia. But they were one of the miracles that offered early glimpses of hope to me at Trinity. Ian enthusiastically began to serve our students. He led our chapel services with his classical brilliance and became a vital part of my early Leadership Team.

At the same time, I was made painfully aware that the College lacked a senior administrator. There was no Vice President of Administration, just a disgruntled staff and a part time gentleman who would fly in for a few days every two weeks or so. I knew we needed another glimmer of hope.

I have always trusted the little nudges and prompts that Carol feels God is giving her. Again and again, she suggested that I should contact Winston Titus. Winston and Candyce were the pastors of the local church in Ellendale. Beyond that, I knew almost nothing about them. So, in my defense I was understandably hesitant about reaching out to offer Winston a job. If only I had known.

Winston & Candyce Titus

Only a very few times in a lifetime do people of extraordinary ability and character cross our paths. I am grateful for several. Winston is one of those – and then some. Capable, full of integrity and overflowing with amazing relational skills. Add to that one of the sharpest senses of humor you can imagine, and you have the God-given gift that he is. Complimenting him at every level is his outstanding wife Candyce. Quiet and assuming, but capable in every way. Little did I realize at the time that God was about to give us one of the most precious and needed gifts imaginable.

Eventually Carol persuaded me, and I made the call. I asked Winston to join me in this scary adventure to serve as Vice President of Finance and Administration. I was delighted when he accepted, and so we began serving together at about the same time.

Ian, Winston and I formed the Leadership Team for our very vulnerable College. Whether it was because things were so bleak, or just that around the table was so much intelligence and wit, I am not sure. But we laughed and laughed. I remember those meetings so fondly. Ian's creative turn of phrase, Winston's amazing wit and sense of humor all combined to help us navigate almost insurmountable challenges. Week by week we confronted the bad news of discovering that multiple invoices had not been entered onto the system making us unaware of the scope of the financial problems. With forensic determination Winston and Candyce set about getting things in order. I have no idea how many phone calls Winston made, but somehow one month melted into the next and we were still paying salaries, feeding the students and slowly clawing our way back from a deep, dark hole.

Please understand as you read this that the situation we uncovered is typical of many struggling institutions. As issues arise desperate measures are adopted. They either result in a sad outcome and the closure of the institution or, as in our case, a series of God-given miracles and rediscovered vision. It is unnecessary and wrong to try to lay blame. These situations sometimes develop over years. They are the accumulation of events and small decisions that, in retrospect, were not the best. Inevitably many people are involved. Should there have been earlier intervention? Probably. Could something else have been done to prevent the dire circumstances we found ourselves in? Maybe. But I decided that it was a present reality and laying blame or finding fault was not going to help. It was true then and it is true now.

Winston came into my office one morning with his characteristically big eyes. I knew he had uncovered some more bad news. Indeed, he had. Apart from the ever-growing secured debt in our mortgage we found that we had short term, unsecured debts that amounted to hundreds of thousands of dollars. Kind friends of the College had loaned money to help get through a pay day or an urgent end-of-month expense. Being new to the job, none of us were aware of these accumulated loans.

One of these debts was in the amount of fifty thousand dollars. A kind business couple who lived in eastern Montana had given the loan and were justifiably wanting to know what our plans were about repaying it. This was the bad news Winston had come to convey. He and I slumped into one of the chairs in my office. Was this going to be the blow that would take us down?

Instinctively I knew that the first decision to make was the one that demanded character and courage. I asked Winston for a check for five thousand dollars. Knowing full well that this was nearly unaffordable and would place other payments on hold, Winston graciously agreed to my request. I recall with absolute clarity the letter I wrote to these kind friends. I apologized for not repaying the amount sooner. (Of course, I did not even know that we owed it!) I went on to let them know of the check enclosed and assured them that this was "my earnest" that all would be repaid. With my heart in my mouth, I walked down the corridor, attached a stamp to the envelope and mailed it.

About ten days later a letter was passed to me and in the upper left-hand corner was the name and address of the couple that I had sent the check to. I braced myself for an unpleasant read. I knew that they had every reason in the world to express their distress at our tardiness in repaying the debt in full. Perhaps there was a demand for immediate payment. Either way, I did not open the envelope with anything else but trepidation. As I opened the letter to my surprise, our check fell out and landed on my desk. It had a bold line drawn right through it. Perhaps they were telling me not to insult them in this way and please forward the whole amount. Tears welled in my eyes as I read on. They were returning the check. They were grateful for my letter. Then they informed me that they were cancelling the loan in its entirety and wished me God's blessing on my leadership of Trinity Bible College. Something in the invisible world seemed to break in that moment. Here was another glimmer of hope. This was a miracle, and I knew it. These wonderful friends have gone on to send us gifts from time to time. They will never fully know what their kindness achieved that day. It was the beginning of hope and breakthrough.

Ian – what a gift. Winston - another God-given help and now this first of many miracles. I began to believe for bigger and greater things.

The Davidson Hall story features several times in this book, but it played a vital role in these very early days. Whether it was our upbringing in a former British colony or years spent living in England, the little rituals and rhythms of daily life have always been important to us. These include a coffee break mid-morning. In England they used to refer to this time as "elevenses". Then there is afternoon tea. It seemed natural to me to enquire on our first day in office where the staff and faculty met for morning coffee. I was astonished to discover that they did not meet. Somewhat confounded, I then asked where social gatherings took place and was even more astounded to discover that such a space did not even exist. I knew this needed correcting as soon as possible.

Hugely influential in our decision to accept the challenge to lead Trinity was the irrepressible Sam Johnson. It is difficult to overestimate the contribution he has made to the current well-being of the College. He would visit often, offer advice and always faithfully help in garnering friends to assist us. As we were walking around the campus, I shared my dismay at having no place where the staff and faculty could meet together socially. Worse still, there seemed to be no obvious place available. Eventually we made our way over to the sad, locked up building known as Davidson Hall. On the first floor to the south of the building were the dusty remains of what had once been an elegant student lounge. Sam and I decided we were going to make good use of this space. Sam recruited some painters, I managed to find two old window air conditioners and we worked through the summer to make the place look decent. We had power, but no heating apart from the two window units. There was no running water. We furnished the room with an eclectic array of furniture. We asked our local furniture store owner for a good deal on everything that had been on his show room floor for a long period of time. Remarkably, it all seemed to match. Carol and I carefully arranged the furniture into conversational groups, we found lamps for ambiance and stood back proudly looking at the transformation of this tired old room.

As the new semester began, we carried two large pots of coffee across the open space between the cafeteria and the new room that we had called "The Commons" after taking a vote among the staff. I became somewhat obsessive about the importance of making time on a daily basis to meet together. It was important to me (It still is!) that everyone - janitors, facilities services personnel, administration and faculty gather together, laugh and enjoy half an hour of fellowship every day. For some it was a struggle. It seemed disruptive, but I persisted. Each year during our annual Vision Day I would stress the importance of that space. It is now an accepted part of our daily lives. For me it is even more than that. As I show visitors around and take them into what is now an exquisite room, I often feel my throat tightening and emotion rising. I have said it a thousand times and more. That room healed our College. The Commons was an important part of hope and courage returning. The glimmer of hope was growing brighter.

The Commons, present day.

Glimmers of hope continued to come through the kind people whom God brought into our lives. Roland and Judy Dudley had served as missionaries for years in Europe. We first met Roland decades ago while he was on a short visit to South Africa. Later we had more interaction when I was leading the European Pentecostal Theological Association and Roland was President of the European Theological Seminary in Belgium. Now they were serving as Missionaries in Residence at Trinity. In fact, Roland was instrumental in arranging our first visit to Ellendale.

Now he became another special gift. Not only was their home always open to Carol and me, but he began to mentor and coach me in matters related to college governance. Everything I knew paled in the light of what he knew. He helped me structure the College around core work processes and enabled me to bring leadership to our Board as we emerged from difficult times. I will forever be grateful to Roland for his wisdom and insight.

It was Roland who introduced us to his home church in Virginia. They had regularly sent missions groups out from the church, and North Dakota became their focus for a number of years. We have had multiple teams serve us over the years, but it is this group that deserves special mention. They came when we had virtually no resources, buildings were in a very poor state of repair and most of our projects seemed to lack any viability due to a lack of resources. Just like the returned check mentioned earlier, this group broke through in the unseen world. I remember speaking to them one morning in our chapel. I chose as my subject thoughts surrounding the work of God in "spaces and places." Throughout the Bible there are special places where God seems to do extraordinary things. Spaces become sacred and special. I thanked them for investing in this special place and asked them to pray that it would become a sacred space where God works.

This group helped us in what seemed to be the most overwhelming project of all. Davidson Hall (where The Commons is located) is an iconic building that sits right in the center of the campus. It is the first building that can be seen as you drive up Main Street. Built with the resources of both State money and Carnegie foundation money in the very early 1900's, it had served as a women's dormitory for over 100 years. Now it was a sad, disintegrating building, and I knew that we had to get it back.

Davidson Hall interior, before renovation.

Bravely we started internal demolition. We discovered that the foundation had shifted due to frost and was now crumbling. Huge hydraulic jacks needed to be brought in, the entire building lifted and enormous steel "I" beams inserted. Our friends from Virginia shared our faith that somehow we could get it back. I walked up to the second floor one warm afternoon. About four miles of data cables were needed to make the building useful as our new central administration building. The task of drilling holes and pulling these wires through was immense. One gentleman was up a ladder, sweating in the heat with wood curls in his hair from the holes he had drilled. I thanked him for his willingness and kindness in serving us. He reached down, extended his hand and introduced himself as Vern. I gave my name and then he mentioned his last name. It was Clark. This was none other than Admiral Vern Clark, one of the most senior military men in the country, and at one time, in command of vast parts of the US Navy. Here he was in Ellendale, working and grimy from the dust of the building, just like all the rest. His service shouted the goodness of God to me. Another glimmer of hope and promise. That group from Virginia played a significant seminal role in the slow but determined progress we were making as a college.

Following a Board of Trustees meeting one of the Board members mentioned a person who attended his church who could possibly help with what was a seemingly insurmountable budget shortfall. I still cringe as I remember those trying Board meetings where the only positive report was my own optimism. But the situation was bleak, and we all knew it. I urged the Board member to introduce me to this gentleman.

Not long after, we drove across the state to have a meal at this Board member's home. He and his wife had arranged for us to meet our new friend and served us a delicious meatball dinner. When we arrived at their home, we discovered that they had invited a couple along with the man they had mentioned. We had no idea as to who they were or what kind of resources they might have. Our inclination was that the nice-looking couple was probably quite affluent. We were not entirely sure about the other gentleman but enjoyed the evening and came to say our goodbyes.

As we left our Board member's home the man who we had just shared a meal with mentioned that he would help us. We were not sure what this meant but were encouraged anyway. Some weeks later one of the largest donations we had ever received arrived in the mail. It was amazing, but it was even more wonderful in that it was unrestricted. This means that it was not designated to any specific project. I completely understand why donors restrict their gifts. At Trinity we are meticulous in our fiduciary responsibility to use funds as intended. However, unrestricted gifts often meet the most challenging of financial needs. This gift did exactly that at a time that it was critically needed.

This is how Jon and Sonya McCreary came into our lives. A few months later I received a call from Jon. I was not sure what he meant when he asked what the ceiling was like. I looked up at the roof of my office quizzically. He then helped me by saying that he wanted to fly in and wondered what the cloud cover was like. Ah, that made more sense!

As it happened his plane was a little too big to land at our little airport in Ellendale. Jon rented a car and drove the 45 miles north arriving in the late morning. I had no idea why he was there but welcomed him and began to show him around.

This gave me the opportunity to verbalize my feeling about Davidson Hall. I remember exactly the sense I had on the cold day on January 19th - the morning we first visited the campus. Leaving the north door of the Student Life Center, I looked up at the forlorn pillars of Davidson Hall standing in their faded glory. It was as though they spoke back at me. They almost mocked me. They seemed to be shouting that they were a physical representation of the current state of the Trinity Bible College. The closest emotion I can describe is one of absolute defiance. It was as though a fist clenched inside my gut and quietly, but with determination I looked back at those pillars and shouted on the inside that if I were ever to be the President, I would determine to get the grand building back one square inch at a time. Giving expression to that defiance we had recruited some of the volunteer teams that I have already mentioned and begun the mammoth task of internal demolition.

I explained all of this to Jon as we made our way around the campus. We passed Carol and I suggested that we should meet at our little, prefabricated home for tea in a short while. Jon and I finished our campus tour and made our way to our home. We always offer guests good tea. Of course, it is properly brewed and made from blended loose tea leaves. The pot is always hot, and we prefer to drink tea from decent bone china cups. As always Carol had set the tray and the kettle was boiling. As I welcomed Jon to our home, I could not help but take a second look at the tray. Somewhat to my dismay we did not have cookies to offer that day. I presumed that it was because Jon's visit was unplanned. Rather, there was a whole plate of valuable and delicious Cadbury's milk chocolate. Carol had invaded my stash of this valuable commodity. I was sure to point out to my guest how fortunate he was.

Teatime came and went, and soon I was walking across the campus to bid Jon farewell. He got into the rental car, rolled down his window and I walked slowly alongside the car as he made his way back towards Main Street. Behind me was Davidson Hall. I thanked Jon for coming although, in the back of my head, I was still not sure why he had gone to all the trouble to fly in. He leaned out of the car, thanked me for the welcome and then informed me that he would give a similar amount of money that he had given the previous year. My heart leapt, I felt the rush of relief and joy all at the same time. Then he pointed to the old, sad building behind me. "We need to get that back as well," he said. Of course, I agreed. He proceeded to promise a large amount of money. I could hardly get the words out - I was so overcome! His commitment that day came to over seven figures and Jon and Sonya have been true to that promise and several since. The glimmer of hope seemed to burst into a bright shining light of hope and prospect.

So, the early despair and hopelessness of a great College struggling on the verge of closure began to fade. The right people were in place. Good internal organizational structures were developing, and the Board of Trustees was beginning to offer good governance. Trustees' committees allowed for the key work processes of the College to be thoroughly and honestly dealt with and signs of health were increasingly evident. Now there were some tangible expressions of the support that we so desperately needed. Could we trust for more? Was this really the start of a season of restoration and rebuilding so that Trinity Bible College and Graduate School could fulfil its mission of training and educating men and women in such a way that they would be ambassadors of Christ's good news in our locality, in our region and around the world? Certainly, it seemed as though this could all be a glorious reality, and Carol and I were ready for the challenge.

Davidson Hall interior, present day.

CHAPTER FIVE

The Prayer Chapel

Prayer – Heart and Center

There were good reasons why the University of North Dakota chose the Ellendale campus at the turn of the 20th Century. First of all, there was an armory on the site. After the Civil War, the federal government built armories around the nation. The idea was to arm the citizenry and prevent the rise of militia groups. The Armory remains a feature on our campus and has recently enjoyed a complete refurbishment. So, the land was already state owned. Another good reason was that Ellendale was almost exactly halfway between Jamestown in the north and Aberdeen, SD, to the south. At the turn of the 20th century this represented almost a day's journey from either of the larger cities. With rapidly expanding farming communities and a desire to develop the southeast of the state, Ellendale was chosen for the University. The University developed a good reputation for training schoolteachers and excelled in manual arts training. Ellendale also happened to be the county seat and boasted a grand courthouse.

The state built several elegant buildings and the Carnegie Foundation contributed generously, as well. Two beautiful buildings with Corinthian columns graced the campus, and several other grand buildings including a French-style academic block and an elegant library were also built. The library was ahead of its time. It boasted (as it still does) four floors of book stacks, wood paneled study booths and a beautiful stained-glass skylight that was almost the size of the main hall.

After a catastrophic fire destroyed two of the buildings, Trinity was able to acquire the campus as I have already explained. One building that was not as elegant as the others was the manual arts building. Originally it included a furnace with a tall brick chimney. The bricks had either turned black from the smoke or had been painted black at some point. No matter which way you looked at the building, it could not hide its industrial use, and was unattractive in every sense. The chimney was demolished, some rooms were repainted and for several years it became the main administrative building. Rumor has it that many a first kiss between students was sneaked under the stairs in that building.

From the beginning I despised that building. It was a huge carbuncle that embarrassed me whenever I was showing guests around. As I began my tenure, we had opened a beautiful, state-of-the art fitness center. Its large windows looked directly at this monstrosity. As far back as 1998 the building had been condemned. One part on the lower level was retained as a classroom but otherwise it was unstable and unsafe. A dank basement ran about half of the building's length and archives stored there were slowly rotting in the damp conditions.

The old administration building was a trial to me. Our house was about 180 paces to the west of the building and every morning as I walked to my office, each one of the paces presented me with the building that I had grown to hate so much. I remember walking that path morning after morning imagining how I might finally get rid of the ugly structure.

Slowly a plan was developing in my mind. My first priority was simply to get rid of the ugly building. Of course, the thought occurred to me that it might be riddled with asbestos and that simply getting a bulldozer to flatten it was not necessarily going to work. Nevertheless, I dreamt daily of the time when this trial to my faith would be demolished. Eventually, I felt I could start talking about what we could do. I suggested to some of the team at Trinity that we could arrange to have the building demolished, replace it with a large concrete slab and erect a few dozen flag poles. I called this idea the "Plaza of the Nations," and boldly pronounced that we would encourage students to meet there and pray for the Gospel to go from our campus to all the nations represented by the flags.

Our project manager at the time took me seriously. (I'm glad someone did!) In fact, he had a cheap computer-aided drawing program on his computer and soon produced a rough drawing of what the plaza might look like. It took a lot of imagination, but it was a good start.

Some months later I was attending the District Conference of the North Dakota Assemblies of God district. I naturally gravitated towards the Trinity booth. It is at events like this that wonderful College representatives meet people, recruit new students, and generally make the work of the College known. I was completely surprised to see the grainy image of the "Plaza of the Nations" prominently displayed on the table in front of our booth. I had no idea that it was public at all. This was just a developing idea, and now it was a picture on display before the nearest of our constituents. Of course, the picture immediately attracted attention. People were enthralled and fascinated, but everyone was quick to tell me that it gets very cold in North Dakota and not many prayer meetings would ever take place around those flagpoles. Most North Dakotans that we know are honest, direct; they speak plainly and let you know exactly what they think. They certainly did that day as they surveyed the computer-generated sketch.

I realized very quickly that my idea was not going to attract much traction, and it was probably wise to drop it completely. But somehow, I could not get the thought of a prayer center right in the heart of our campus out of my mind. For years I had slowly fostered the theological conviction that quiet, reflective practices should be much more a part of the formation process of young men and women in training for ministry and service, whether in the ministry or the workplace. I also developed the conviction that many of the remnants of the Reformation had suppressed our appreciation of beauty, ambiance, and the arts. Reformers were determined to get rid of icons and statues. In their zeal they turned their churches into bland buildings with little or no decoration. It is said that the Puritans even dressed the legs of pianos as they thought they might be suggestive. This legacy continued through the centuries and our early Pentecostal fathers made little or no effort to accommodate the arts.

My thinking has always questioned this. Surely the God of all creation reveals His nature through the splendors of His handywork! All that God makes is beautiful, colorful and speaks of His grandeur. Should we not equally appreciate beautiful things? At the same time, I have always harbored a deep concern that our spirituality is often overly activist and not sufficiently reflective. In a rather primitive way, these two concepts began to coalesce in my mind as I thought about the space that was occupied by the horrible Manual Arts building. Could it be possible that I could trust God for a structure in the middle of our campus that would combine a beautiful space along with a commitment to encourage reflective, prayerful practice among our students? Bit by bit a larger plan began to develop in my heart and mind.

The concept developed by thinking that it might be possible to build a small structure in the middle of what might have been the "Plaza of the Nations." We would call it a prayer chapel and its interior would have some beautiful aesthetic components - perhaps some colored glass windows? Or an over-height ceiling clad in wood? Maybe a slightly unusual shape would help set the building apart.

Let me introduce you to Jim Schroll. He was our Projects Manager at the time. Young, inexperienced but more eager than most. He always was quick to help me interpret the scattered thoughts in my mind. Everything was possible for Jim. He quickly became a trusted confidant in my visionary journey. I would share my ideas and he would tease out the thoughts that I had. We would sometimes sketch our ideas on random pieces of paper.

Someone suggested that if we were to seriously replace the old building, we should think of something more than an understated little building in the middle of a large vacant lot. Perhaps a classroom could be attached. And so, Jim and I set to work. We soon added a classroom to the idea we had for a prayer chapel. Then the idea mutated, and we thought that a classroom on each side of the chapel would work. We would often walk to the old building and pace out what we were thinking. The weather was cold, and the wind was fierce, but we had exciting plans developing.

Eventually, the humble prayer chapel envisioned for the replacement for the Manual Arts building was a concept of a major complex including a sweeping atrium with large glass frontage, several classrooms and, of course a magnificent prayer chapel. It was all so thrilling that the cost seldom entered my mind. I sat with Jim and, using his cheap computer program, we envisioned a beautiful building. It connected to buildings to both the north and the south via wide corridors. There was a beautiful atrium that even included a splendid indoor waterfall. Floor to ceiling windows graced the grand, spacious atrium.

Prayer Chapel exterior, construction phase.

Prayer Chapel exterior, final.

I immediately knew that this was exactly what I had been dreaming. A place that included both aesthetically beautiful and completely functional space. Importantly, there was enough imagery in the architecture to send messages to generations of students. The primary message I wanted to convey was that God creates us not for what we do in the first instance, but for who we are. Thus, the Prayer Center served perfectly because it connected the campus – a perfect image in and of itself. This corridor became, in my mind, the main street of the College. Busy, fast-moving students on a mission to the next class or to get into the Fitness Center would rush down these corridors. Then, there was the tranquil sound of the waterfall, two beautiful glass doors and, as you enter them, a soaring place with an elegant wood paneled ceiling and two brightly colored glass windows. This was a tranquil, quiet, and reflective space. This was the image born in the building that, in the busyness of life, real living is to be found in the quiet, reflective space. Entering the chapel, you cannot help but leave the noise behind and take a deep breath in the simple, quiet yet beautiful space.

Prayer Chapel interior, construction phase.

Prayer Chapel interior, final.

Very quickly the excitement of vision turned to the reality of budget. I realized that this was a huge project by anyone's standards. We found an architect who was prepared to help us develop the plans with no upfront cost. Of course, I knew that the meter was already ticking and that all this work would need to be paid for one day. It took several attempts to describe the steeple well enough for the architect to eventually draw it. There were practical considerations such as classroom size, needed technology and even furnishings. We added a serving kitchen and the necessary restrooms. I knew that this vision would one day provide an iconic building for Trinity Bible College and Graduate School.

Even more sobering during this time of vision was the fact that the ugly old Manual Arts building was still stubbornly in place. Why did people have to ask the hard questions such as whether asbestos abatement might be required? Were there other hidden costs in just getting rid of the ugly thing? Each time we tried to find out there was another fee involved. Because of Ellendale's location people need to travel long distances to consult or quote. It felt like there were mounting costs and we had not moved beyond an elaborate dream. Almost daily I was reminded that this expensive vision was transpiring in a college that had mounting debt and academic probation that was still suppressing the number of students that we were recruiting. Many of our alumni were not in any way connected to us. It seemed obvious that the two sides of the ledger were not going to balance. An audacious dream and the harsh realities of an institution in financial and structural trouble did not seem reconcilable.

I resorted to the same strategy that Carol and I had used in every similar situation. We spent long hours discussing our motives, goals and objectives. We checked our hearts as to why we were ambitious for this project. We prayed, and then cautiously shared the idea with trusted friends. This simple process has served us well through many years. We have added our own little rituals. Inevitably, there must be a good cup of brewed tea and preferably a slab of delicious chocolate. Then the discussion between us will go on for hours and by the end, nothing seems impossible.

The Prayer Center project was no different. The vision was in place, its theological reason for being was soundly established, and on a practical level, we really needed the space. As we discussed and prayed, prayed and discussed, I slowly began to develop a sense that there was one couple that I needed to talk to. I did not know them very well. About a year earlier our family had visited us in North Dakota and I really wanted Ty, our little grandson who was about three at the time, to ride in a combine harvester. I knew of a farmer with vast fields north of where we lived and so reached out to him. Soon, Ty and I were riding up and down the rows harvesting bushel upon bushel of soybeans. The day ended at Dairy Queen – of course! And so, a friendship with Reuben and Clarice Liechty was begun, and we continued to develop that friendship through every means possible. Occasional texts, a few phone calls, and meals together from time to time. These dear people have become some of our most faithful and kindest friends in the world.

At the time our relationship was just developing, but I felt certain that I needed to talk to them. Carol had a speaking engagement and it worked out perfectly for me to drop her off and then visit Clarice and Reuben. We enjoyed a cup of coffee together and then, with clammy hands, my heart beating and butterflies in my stomach, I went to my car and retrieved an early version of the plans for the Prayer Center. I had practiced my speech a hundred times. I briefly explained what the project was, showed them the concept drawing and then, before my courage failed me, went straight to the point. Would they please be the anchor donors? Reuben cut straight to the chase. How much? It was then that I made a mistake that I tend to make often. I understated the amount. I told them that I thought we needed about $300,000.00. Reuben's response was immediately to say that it was "$500,000.00 then?" Of course, I agreed with him. Clarice said nothing. I had no idea if our meeting had been a good one or not. I knew they were faithful friends but could not determine if they were ready to be generous donors.

A few weeks went by, and Carol and I left for the United Kingdom to fulfil several preaching and teaching commitments. Our time began in Cambridge. We love this ancient university town with its grand academic buildings set along the river Cam. King's College stands out. Built by the notorious Henry VIII, it still is magnificent over five centuries later. You can meander along miles of pathways either to the "fronts" or the "backs" of the many colleges and residence halls. Of course, there is always time to find a quaint tearoom and stop for a while and enjoy some fresh baked scones, or a tea cake, or a custard slice or all three!

After completing our commitment in Cambridge, we had ministry and teaching commitments in the granite city of Scotland, Aberdeen. On our way some of our former students had been very generous and had booked us into a small, boutique hotel in the heart of the Lake District northwest England. The Lakes have always been one of our favorite regions. The stories of Beatrix Potter and the poems of William Wordsworth were all a result of this spectacular scenery. It was early spring, and the first blossoms were weighing down the branches of the trees. Every step opened new vistas in this beautiful part of the world. The lakes themselves are spectacular - long, deep, grand! The hills dotted with sheep still carrying their winter coats add to the enlivening on the senses. Long, meticulously laid stone walls run clear over the hills. Lanes are quaint and narrow, and every color and hue seem exaggerated. We drank it all in. This was a tonic for our souls, and we were determined to enjoy every minute. With Trinity never far from our hearts and mind, the days passed with long walks, quiet meanders along country paths and long stops in delightful villages. The weather was kind to us as well.

The little hotel was quintessentially British. A Victorian building with fireplaces in each room, typically minute bathrooms, floral carpets, and striped wallpaper. We enjoyed the full English breakfast that is always an expected part of a stay in a small country hotel. For some reason there is always a bowl of canned orange segments. They are not too bad but are a poor substitute for the real thing. Then there is a cereal of some kind or another. But both are a distraction for the real breakfast. A plate comes to the table still steaming and loaded to the very edges. There is thick cut bacon nicely grilled. Always a good sausage – in the Lakes it must be Cumberland sausage. It is worth traveling to England just for a breakfast that includes Cumberland sausage. It is served in a small roll beautifully browned and caramelized on both sides. There is normally a slice of fried tomato and the eggs, served anyway you like. Oh, let's not forget the baked beans! Always baked beans running with rich tomato juice, sometimes served on toast, but normally they fill the plate with their own color and flavor. Tucked neatly onto the edge of the plate are two triangular slices of fried bread. It simply would not be an English breakfast without fried bread. As you indulge, you quietly promise yourself that you will not need to eat for the rest of the day. In reality, the beautiful pastries on display in the village coffee shop are enough to make you break that commitment before lunch.

The day before I had received an unusual text from a member of my team back in Ellendale. Our friends Clarice and Reuben had arranged to visit the campus and review the project. I was not sure that I liked what I heard. After all, this was my vision, and I was the one who knew the most about the project. Could they not wait to visit until we returned from the UK? Obviously, they could not and so a visit was planned. I so hoped that I had communicated enough to the team at Trinity. Would they represent the project like I would? I had my doubts, but there was little that I could do. Somehow, as we explored the beautiful English countryside, this meeting was always on my mind.

We enjoyed a leisurely breakfast: bacon, egg, sausage – always sausage, and finished with toast made using bread from the local baker and topped with butter from a local dairy and the best marmalade. A good cup of tea poured from a china pot completed the scrumptious feast. We left the table and made our way back to our quaint room to prepare for the day. Climbing the narrow stairs, I felt my phone buzz in my shirt pocket. We had managed to escape the tyranny of always looking at our phones, but this was an unusual hour. The first part of the text appeared on my screen – "miracle of stupendous proportions…" I decided to leave opening the text until we were inside our room. We paused at the end of the bed, Carol snuggled up to my shoulder and we opened the text. In it was the amazing news that the finances for the chapel had been provided.

I received the news on how this all transpired upon my return to North Dakota. That day that Reuben and Clarice drove to Ellendale, they had already decided that they would like to fund this beautiful building. After some discussion with the Trinity team, they walked to the end of the hall and out into the sunshine to survey the old Administration building. Upon returning to the little conference room, they informed our team that they were not only going to give sufficient for the chapel, but were, in fact, going to fund the entire project.

As we read of this news emotion welled up within us. Carol and I embraced, unashamedly shed tears, and then quietly bowed our heads and thanked our loving Heavenly Father for kind friends and for honoring our vision. Throughout the day waves of emotion swept over us. At times it was an emotion of immense relief and at times it was the ecstatic feeling of expectation of this beautiful building in the heart of the campus. Each time I walk the hallway and make my way into the beautiful atrium the same emotions rise within me.

Prayer Chapel Atrium

And so began the incredible journey that would stretch all of us and cement a friendship with Reuben and Clarice that is profound and deep to this day. Plans were sent back and forth to the architect. Long meetings were held to make sure we all agreed on progress. The Liechtys would often make the sixty-mile journey to Ellendale to ensure that all was on track.

As Spring slowly came back to the northern plains our students left for their spring break. Carol and I returned from leading a student team and made our way to the southwest of North Dakota to speak in a church there. It was there that I received some devastating news. Three of our young men had traveled to a western state for their break. Coming home along the interstate there was a thick mist. For some unknown reason a truck was stationary in the fast lane. The young men's car plowed into the stopped vehicle. Two were rushed to hospital in Bismarck and I quickly made my way there to see them in the Intensive Care ward. But Cameron Bird had been killed instantly. Cameron came from a great Christian family in Texas. He was an outstanding young African American student who had enriched our community with his sense of fun and vibrant personality. He was also a great athlete. The news of his death brought deep pain to the Trinity community.

About a week later the students organized a memorial service for Cameron. With a broken heart I sat in our chapel and mourned the loss of a precious young life. As the service concluded we exited the chapel, and each person was handed a white balloon. A few said words of comfort and remembrance and then we all let the balloons free to fly to the cry of "fly high Birdman" (Cameron's nickname). I watched and then realized that the wind was blowing the balloons upward but towards the huge red steel frame of the Prayer Center that was now several months into construction. That scene will forever be etched in my mind. I fought back the tears as I saw the white balloons ascend past the new steeple and away into the sky. I prayed then as I do now for every one of our students. "God, would you grant that they would love and serve you all their days."

As the building progressed, we began to talk with Clarice and Reuben about the naming of classrooms. Quickly they responded by saying that one should be named after the first Superintendent of the Assemblies of God North Dakota District. And so, the classroom to the north of the building is called the "Herman G Johnson Classroom." The other one was to be named in memory of their daughter. So, the other classroom will forever be the "Gwendolyn Ruth Liechty Classroom." I tend to pause for just a moment each time I walk that hall. I look into the spacious, well-equipped classrooms, look at the signage above and recall the tender way in which the request was made to name them.

There was one more requirement that was not up for negotiation. At first it seemed unusual, but every day since I have been grateful. It was that in prominent letters on the outside of the building the words "Safe in the Arms of Jesus" were to be written. These words are particularly poignant to Clarice and Reuben. They are the line of a hymn sung at Gwen's funeral. Now they are deeply meaningful to me. It is absolutely fitting that we should commend every one of our students to be safe in the arms of Jesus. A student going to be a pastor? May they be safe in the arms of Jesus. A missionary? May they likewise be safe in the arms of Jesus. And the same for schoolteachers, coaches and businesspeople who graduate from Trinity. I point those words out to everyone who visits our campus. They stand out prominently on the front of the Prayer Center.

Eventually the building was completed, furniture was purchased and installed, and a great crowd gathered for the dedication. Doug Clay, who was a member of the Executive Leadership of the Assemblies of God at the time and is now the General Superintendent, was invited to be the speaker at the dedication of the building. What a great day that was.!

And so, the Prayer Center, its sweeping atrium, state of the art classrooms, and beautiful chapel stand in the heart of our campus. May this iconic building speak to generations to come of the faithfulness of God and of the need for a strong, reflective faith to precede any of our efforts to make Christ known around the world.

CHAPTER SIX

Pack your Bags, GO Trips, and Graduate School

Reimagining Christian Higher Education

As we began our journey into Christian higher education in the US, several things quickly alerted me. One was the escalating cost of an education and the high debt burden that many students were graduating with. I understood the accounting but was distressed at the consequences. My reading and observation made me concerned. Some economists suggest that the massive debt burden carried by American students is a bubble that is ready to burst. It is front and center in political debate but seems to be a football thrown about with no one prepared to catch it and do something with it. Added to this was my deep concern that this problem was exaggerated in the case of young people wanting to enter ministry or missionary service. How could they plan a career with large debts hanging over their heads?

My PhD studies had caused me to dive deeply into the

abundance of literature related to theological education. So, I was familiar with much of the higher education world. But another thing that struck me was how long some students were taking to make their way through to a first degree. In fact, the national average was creeping up, and a significant number of students were taking as long as six years to graduate. All the time they were accumulating debt.

As an educator I wanted to be a part of the solution, not the problem. How could we give young people a great start that would enable them to navigate life and make good choices along the way? Should everyone go on to higher education? In the diverse world in which we live we need people of every type – mechanics and farmers, nurses and doctors, ministers and lawyers. For some, a classical liberal arts first degree might not be the best way to prepare for their future. These, and a multitude of other thoughts, invaded my mind in the early stages of transitioning into the US higher education world.

Bit by bit a concept for a partial solution began to enter my mind. What if we could use the best that a Christian college has to offer – classes, administrative infrastructure, security, and then add a high level of mentoring and travel that would broaden perspectives and produce rapid maturity and make it all available in a package deal for young people? What if we could instill serious life skills into an impressionable young person before bad habits are developed? Things like good financial management, relational skills, and even personal disciplines like eating well and regular exercise? Could we add such a program to a college? Could we even structure the program to include some college credit? By now I was dreaming and imagining with no idea of whether it would be possible or not.

It was thus that PackYourBags was born. I imagined a program that would have at least four major components. Firstly, there would be a life skills component. Simple, yet vital, life lessons would be imparted and then reinforced by a trip somewhere. We soon found at least two such trips. One was to serve people living in the challenging environment of a Native American reservation. The other was to join hands with a ministry that served the homeless and had developed a dynamic poverty simulation experience for young people. By spending twenty-four hours living with the immense challenges of homelessness young people could rapidly learn not to dismiss poverty in a casual, thoughtless way.

We also worked at what we called a "ministry phase." The intention was to help young people articulate their faith. It seems obvious that culture shift requires ways to articulate the eternal good news message without cliché or repetitive rhetoric. We really wanted to find at least some of these ways. This phase ends with students choosing one of several tracks in places as far away as South Africa, India, or the Philippines.

PackYourBags Students Abroad.

A third phase was equally important to me. It was simply a Bible phase. The level of biblical illiteracy among young American students is now well documented. Could we be a part of the solution? This phase would be completed with a trip to Israel. Kayaking on the Jordan river or taking a jeep safari up the Golan heights would form an exciting part of discovering the Land of the Book.

Finally, there would be an exit phase. With careful mentoring, supportive prayer, and good information, we would seek to advise students on the next steps in their life's journey. Of course, there were teething problems. Thankfully the students were largely unaware of the background struggles. What courses would be available? Could financial aid be made accessible? One by one we worked through the issues and now, several years later PackYourBags is deeply rooted as a part of our offerings. Amazing young people have come through the program - many going on to complete a four-year degree and complete their studies at Trinity. Several have served this program with distinction, and we are all better for their service.

I am so glad that we have been able to integrate a program like this into the wider curriculum offered at Trinity. It speaks loudly to a commitment to help young people journey into adulthood with skills that will serve them well. Good manners are important. Perspective in life is priceless. To be mentored, challenged, and presented with the prospect of living a noble and useful life is what we stand for. I feel a warm glow inside each time I see our PackYourBags team of students.

If introducing PackYourBags was stretching for our college, my next passion would prove even more so. My entire educational theory is based upon the concept of preparing heads, hearts and hands. In other words, a ministry training without a strong connectedness to serving becomes nothing more than an exercise in dead orthodoxy. Somehow, I always instinctively knew this, and am glad that I have been able to implement practical training opportunities in every institution that I have led.

Years ago, Carol and I led a team back to South Africa. We served a very needy community near to where we used to live. I always love these times. Spending time in the company of fun-loving students has got to be one of the greatest perks of my job. Our team was just this – fun loving, happy and carefree. We traveled from our lodgings early one morning, and one of the leaders of the ministry we were working with met us. It seemed as though there was not a lot organized as far as tasks were concerned, but it was suggested that maybe we could paint a room for a young girl. At just twelve years old, this little girl had been orphaned. She lost her parents to the scourge of HIV/AIDS. A family in the village had taken her in and added a crude room to the side of their house. It was made of corrugated iron mainly and was grey and dismal. We were shown the room, agreed to paint it, and a small group of students made their way to a nearby building supply store to buy paint. They asked the storekeeper if he had any discounted paint. They were delighted when he informed them that he had specially made a batch for a customer who had never returned to buy the paint. What he did not tell them was that it was the brightest canary-yellow color you have ever seen. But it was going at a price they could not refuse.

So, they returned to the house with an abundant supply of paint. The little girl was away at school and had no idea that her room was being painted. As is almost inevitable with a group of students, it was hard to keep them on task. They painted crazy designs on the walls. Then they all wrote their names as though they were emerging Picasso's. Eventually I managed to persuade them, and they finally got down to the task at hand. The walls and even the roof were all painted bright yellow. We cleaned things up, rearranged the meager furniture and waited for the little girl to return from school.

It was just like the ultimate reveal. She walked in with her hands over her eyes. When she was told to open her eyes, her face lit up! Then tears flowed freely, and all the time she was asking if this was really her room. Others began to fight back the tears. The happy labors of a student team combined with a gallon of discounted yellow paint changed a little girl's life. Equally, a team of students who had started the day in a carefree, jovial way instantly knew that they would never be the same again. Seeing the emotion and joy on that little girl's face impacted them deeply.

This, and literally hundreds of similar stories, made persuaded me that I really wanted a mission trip program at Trinity. In fact,

I wanted every student, in every year of their study to go on a mission trip. I wanted the classroom discussions to be put into practice. And, just as important, I wanted the impact of serving in a needy community to condition discussions in theology classes. Somewhat naively, I proposed that we should start a "GO Trip" requirement for all our students.

I soon learned that this was not going to be easy. How much time would be lost from the classroom, and how could that be made up? Who was going to coordinate these trips and handle the huge logistical burden they would create? Then there were the demands of various athletic programs, and much more. At times there was outright opposition to the idea altogether. Why not put all these grand concepts into a summer program and not mess with the semester?

About the time I was trying to get Go Trips established at Trinity, a Missionary-in-Residence joined Trinity's faculty. Dave Jacob, his lovely wife Angie, and their five children had been serving in Northern Asia as missionaries under appointment with the Assemblies of God World Mission. An arrangement known as "Missionary in Residence" program brought them to Trinity. This is an excellent program that deserves just a moment of mention. Often missionaries find themselves between assignments. The pressure on them during these times is immense. Questions like where to base, or how to educate their children can have difficult and complex answers. So, an opportunity exists whereby these families can serve at a college or university for a time before returning to the mission field. One of the weaknesses of this otherwise great arrangement is the lack of understanding on the part of supporters of the missionary family.

Dave and Angie have faced the loss of support as they have journeyed with us but have done so much to serve the cause of mission. I asked him to set up an office directly across the hall from my office. Although he had many responsibilities, I charged him with one additional area of oversight. It was to work with faculty and administration to make my vision of GO trips a reality.

It seemed like almost every other day he ran into one obstacle or another. None of these challenges surprised me. Things change slowly in educational institutions. We began with all freshmen and sophomores taking a trip. Eventually Dave's patience and diplomacy paid off, and within a few short years the entire College closed just before spring break, and student teams took off around the country and around the world.

Now we could not imagine Trinity Bible College and Graduate school without GO trips. Faculty and staff begin to plan trips during the summer and early fall. They reach out to churches, Dream Centers and other ministries and find out what would be involved in bringing a team. Then budgets are set and a price for the trip announced. Several chapels are devoted entirely to publicizing the available GO Trips. It is always exciting! You can feel the expectancy in the air as someone shares about an opportunity to serve with a Trinity alumnus in Spain or go to help needy families in Bolivia. We have gone to northern Asia and Southern Africa. Australia and India have received teams, plus New Orleans, Las Vegas, Charlotte, Texas, Missouri, and Los Angeles. And there are more!

Go Trip Student Abroad

In order not to exclude anyone, we serve ministries close to the College as well. It often seems as though God compensates for the lack of travel by giving exceptional opportunities to these teams that serve regionally. A student serving on a regional team happened to visit Walmart in a nearby town during the GO Trip. Somehow, he was attracted to a man sitting alone in his pickup truck. A conversation began, and slowly the man's sad story emerged. A disappointment in his life led to disillusionment and eventually choices that caused him to become completely dysfunctional. On this day his life seemed particularly hopeless, and he had no idea what would happen next. Enter a Trinity student on a Regional GO Trip. Hope was offered, prayer was invited and, before the encounter came to an end, the man had completely dedicated his life to Christ and was on a new trajectory. Of course, contact was kept, and we believe that this was one of those many remarkable encounters that God creates for people who deliberately disrupt the rhythm of their lives to serve Him. That is exactly what the Trinity community does every year. Every student in every year of their studies allows disruption in their year in order to be available in a concentrated way for God to show His grace and love through them. This is our GO Trip program. May it always be a feature of the Trinity experience.

I was so committed to GO Trips that I began to structure the Leadership Team at Trinity to include someone to spearhead these many practical experiences. I began to enquire of my colleagues in Christian Higher Education and discovered that there was virtually nobody in the senior leadership echelons of any other institution that fully represented experiential learning. Well, we did it. I created the role of "Vice President of Experiential Learning." The Board of Trustees enthusiastically supported me, and before long, I had recruited Garrett Freier to take this role. Up until this point he had served as Director of Student Ministries, but it made sense to consolidate all our practical ministry programs under his leadership. The PackYourBags program, GO Trips and all our internships, summer ministry programs and weekly service programs all are a part of his responsibilities. Recently we discovered that there was a team traveling from Trinity on average every 4.2 days. Thousands of miles are driven each year, multiple countries are visited and literally thousands and thousands of ministry hours are given through the experiential learning initiatives of Trinity.

Graduate School

If digging out of a deep debt burden, trying to motivate a disheartened faculty, and introducing radical new initiatives were not enough, I also wanted to begin a fully functioning Graduate School at Trinity. During our years in the United Kingdom, we had witnessed the huge impact that graduate level study had on ministry leaders. Many whose ministry had become somewhat stagnant found new impetus and vision. In fact, one of the most gratifying parts of our ministry in higher education was the development of innovative post graduate programs that provided continuing education opportunities for those in Christian leadership and ministry. We were honored and humbled to be a major part of the development of leaders across Africa, all around Europe, the US, the UK and even in distant places like South India and South East Asia.

It seemed only natural that we should do the same at Trinity. However, there were some major roadblocks to this otherwise good idea. The first was that, just months prior to me assuming the responsibility of President at Trinity, the College had suffered some major setbacks in terms of accreditation. A combination of factors had all come together to force our accreditors to place us under academic probation. This is a very severe censure indeed. Worse still, it is a public censure. This means that every piece of advertising, our website and any other public document had to show that the College was under probation. Additionally, I had to make an appearance before the Council on Accreditation each year and give an account of our operations.

It was a very formal event. At a given time, I was summoned by a rather severe gentleman (I lightheartedly referred to him as the "Sargent-at arms"), and then marched into a room filled with equally severe people. These commissioners have a huge responsibility. They are answerable to the US Department of Education, as well as all the other institutions that they accredit.

During my first appearance I was asked to give account for how Trinity was managing the probation. I thought I had given a very positive account, and that they would hopefully soften their position. I was asked to leave the room and then marched back in about ten minutes later. I was shocked to hear the finding – probation would remain. I returned to the College a little disheartened but determined that we would turn this situation around.

With probation hanging over our heads, it seemed a particularly inopportune time to talk about a new initiative as grandiose as the launch of a Graduate School. Carol and I had long conversations, and we both felt that we should at least inquire as to what would be involved in establishing a Master of Arts program at Trinity. We spent a short time with the leadership of our accreditors and finally mustered sufficient courage to ask the important question. Would an application for substantive change to introduce a master's program even be considered? To our delight and surprise, we were told that not only would it be seriously considered but that, with our background and experience, we should consider starting the process as soon as possible. Without hesitation I asked Carol to lead the charge. She was typically hesitant at first, but soon rose to the challenge with incredible determination.

Carol gathered a small team around her. She brought her experience of a research-based program familiar to most who study in a European context and slowly, but surely, adjusted it to fit an American credit-based system. Soon a detailed document was produced, and application was made to accredit a Master of Arts in

Missional Leadership. Years before we had been the first people in the world, as far as we know, to use this nomenclature. So, we felt it would be a good fit for the degree that we now wanted to offer. It was a degree in practical theology that would allow flexibility and specialization so that students could research ministry-specific fields that would serve their call and ministry.

I met with one of our most generous donors at the back of a Denny's restaurant. I knew that launching an initiative as bold as a Graduate School would stretch our meager financial resources. I simply asked if he could help introduce me to some potential new friends who might share our vision. Without hesitation he stated that he and his wife would carry the full amount needed for the launch. I was quite overwhelmed! What seemed like a ridiculous proposition only weeks earlier was all starting to transpire. We had received encouragement from our accreditors, Carol had accepted the challenge to lead the Graduate School and now we had sufficient funds to launch the enterprise as soon as the Commission on Accreditation accepted our proposal.

Twelve brave women and men formed the first intrepid class. Oh, we worked hard! Course content, delivery methods and classroom content were all discussed at length. Then when the first students arrived, we made sure there were bowls and bowls of chocolates and candies. Constant good quality coffee was always available along with anything else that we could think of that would help impress these amazing people who were committing their post graduate education to us.

A little less than three years later, our first post graduate students joined the celebrations at our Graduation and rose to accept their Master of Arts degrees. Amongst them were the District Superintendent of an Assemblies of God district, the Assistant Superintendent of that same district as well as some of our own staff. Also among the number were Dwight and Nadine Sandoz. They had been serving as the District Superintendents of the Nebraska District of the Assemblies of God. Dwight's obvious passion was for the leaders of rural churches. In fact, he had committed a major part of his work to conducting a thorough empirical research project in which he examined several particularly successful rural churches around our region. What he found astonished and enthused him. Rural churches could have huge impact in the communities they seek to serve.

The impact of his research led Dwight to approach us about launching a new degree. The suggestion was that we structure a unique degree specializing in rural ministry. So, while continuing their studies with a PhD degree program, Dwight and Nadine became adjunct faculty members of the Graduate School at Trinity, and we launched the Master of Arts in Rural Ministry degree. We searched far and wide to find similar degrees. We found none. In fact, as far as we know, this degree remains the first and only graduate degree offering a specialization for those committed to ministry in rural communities. The basic architecture of the program allows students to have immersive experiences based at one or other of the churches or ministries that Dwight had discovered during his studies. As with all the Trinity MA degrees, the program concludes with a major capstone thesis project which allows the students to research something that is ministry specific to themselves. It is enthralling! Stories of new initiatives, rekindled ministry passions and innovative new strategies being discovered abound. We have watched in awe and amazement as these brave women and men have completed their studies, some under extraordinarily challenging circumstances, and then walked the line at graduation. They are heroes each one. Dwight and Nadine have served our rural ministers well by highlighting their unique context and providing an advanced study program for them.

At about the same time as we were launching the very innovative rural ministries program, we began conversations about another program that seemed even more innovative and stretched our thinking in every way. For years people had been fascinated with the many friendships that Carol and I enjoyed around the world. Having lived on four continents and having had the joy of helping people all around the world access good ministry education and training, we know people and have friends in a lot of places. Over the years we have visited these friends and spoken in dozens of churches and conferences. Could we now lean on some of these friendships and develop a post-graduate program that could bring the global context together into a valuable learning experience?

This began a personal theological journey for me. For a long while I had felt uncomfortable with the traditional seminary curriculum that had most of its roots in the systematized theological system established during and immediately after the Reformation. Having helped dozens of African leaders and struggled internally with the awful oppressiveness of the Apartheid system in the land of my birth, I wrestled to reconcile so much of my own theological education with the realities of life in the two thirds world. Western arrogance grieved me deeply, especially when it was dished up with paternalistic attitudes and intertwined with theological thought that was almost indistinguishable from contemporary Western cultural lifestyles and values. What if we could learn from those who had forged their theological thoughts on the anvil of the post-colonial realities that had consumed so many struggles and battles during the second half of the twentieth century? What if we could get immersed in a religiously pluralistic context and evaluate the vibrancy of our faith from within this complex milieu?

These uncomfortable thoughts caused me to dig even deeper. Was it possible that many of the theological thoughts and systems that we use to describe our spiritual experience in the West had, in fact, ignored some of the dramatic events of the Twentieth century? I began to read strangely disturbing histories of those nations that had been the custodians of various Christian traditions and had then allowed themselves to be thrown into the cauldron of the Great War (1914-1918). At least seven kings of nations often thought to be Christian lost their thrones after the war. Millions of lives were sacrificed on the altar of arrogance and the expansion of Empire. I read of the intense spirituality of the Tsar of Russia and the privileged position of the clergy of the Russian Orthodox church, and the violence that brought them down and replaced their power with the atheism of the Bolsheviks. The vast Austro-Hungarian Empire virtually disappeared after the Great War. So-called Christian Europe abused its power and the world reeled as its young men were killed in unheard of numbers. Empires fell, including the great Ottoman Empire and a new world emerged. Yet, we seldom spoke of these things in the hallowed halls of our seminaries.

Soon a logical trajectory developed in my reading and my thinking. The collapse of Empires brought the incredible injustices of the colonial era into perspective, and liberation movements were spawned around the world. Rampant secular humanism filled the void left by the collapse of Christendom, and classical postmodern thought was developed in the classrooms of elite universities. Vast migrations of people took place in the decades after the Second World War. In Europe people from across the former colonies called for opportunity and many were given opportunities to relocate to Europe to meet the labor shortages that the wars had brought about. As they moved into their new host nations, they brought a plethora of religious practices and ideas, and the collision of these with the Christian traditions of Europe produced the inevitable struggles of religious pluralism, fairness, and equity. And yet these complex issues did not find their way into our conservative seminaries by and large. Was it possible that we, having experienced so many of these forces, could develop a program that could evaluate all these realities in a gracious and objective way and explore meaningful ways to make Christ known in the complex world of the 21st Century? This was how our MA in Global Theology was born.

The stories emerging from our travels with our students are truly remarkable. We have wept with those that were the victims of the racial policies in South Africa. We have shared the despair of a young mother holding her baby in a Jane Temple in South India desperately hoping that one of her many gods will hear her prayers. We have sat together in the guilded halls of the Victoria and Albert Museum in London and pondered the insidious impact of Empire and how the spirit of Empire still lives within our hearts.

One particularly remarkable event happened when we were in the Middle East. We had taken time to understand global Islam and the impact of the migration of Islamic people around the world. One of the experiences we had been able to arrange was to meet with the editor of the radicalized newspaper of the Muslim Brotherhood. He was clearly uncomfortable but did not pull any punches. He told us of his hatred for everything American. He spoke of the plunder of Islamic lands by greedy Western corporations. We were left in no doubt of his hatred for the very things that we as a team stood for. We responded with grace, and I then told him that it was our practice to ask each student to reflect on what they had heard. He had enough character to be willing to listen to us. One by one our students responded with grace and dignity. They expressed appreciation for his honesty and quietly explained why we held to our faith and world view.

One of our students was a Native American young lady named Julianne. She had progressed to a senior rank in the National Guard, and the entire MA program was in some ways the story of her own life on a global scale. She thanked our Islamic friend for his comments. She then went on to explain that she understood many of his positions. She told how her people had had their land taken by force. She explained the pain that several generations of her people had experienced and how she could easily have anticipated a broken life. Then there was a remarkable moment when she explained that she had chosen the pathway of forgiveness, and that she could do this because she had been forgiven. In sweet tones and succinct words, she described the love of Christ and how He had changed her life. The room dripped with silence. It was such a poignant moment. After what seemed like a long time we moved on and said our goodbyes. I accompanied the man out of the building and thanked him again for his time. He looked at me with penetrating eyes and told me that he had never been in an atmosphere like what he had just experienced. I quietly assured him that we would pray for him. The Christian man who had brought the editor to meet us has reported several times since that his Islamic friend still often comments on his profound experience with our students.

The global pandemic has interrupted some aspects of our graduate studies, but Carol and her team have been flexible and the numbers of people studying with us continues to increase. New MA programs in Chaplaincy and Intercultural Studies have now been added. The various degrees are also available for dual credit for our undergraduate students, and an excellent opportunity is afforded to our students to complete both a BA and a MA in five concentrated years.

As the number of students graduating through our MA degrees grew, the need for further studies began to present itself. As a result, a PhD in Practical Theology was added to the Graduate School. Now students from Asia, Europe, Africa, the Middle East, and across the USA are undertaking their PhD studies at Trinity. What a remarkable story! We take pause from time to time, catch our breath and express our awe and amazement at the faithful God who has made this all possible. Our reach and impact grow day by day.

PackYourBags for those just starting their adult lives, practical ministry opportunities for those completing their studies, and multiple post graduate degrees are all remarkable testimonies of God's goodness to a small school set in the middle of the vast prairies of North America. The grand old hymn "Great is Thy Faithfulness" comes to mind.

But what about that looming threat of academic probation? It continued to be a cloud that hung over us as so many positive things were happening. I returned for my appearance before the Commission on Accreditation during the second year. This time I asked one of our trustees to accompany me. We were duly marched in as in the previous year. Again, a severe panel of people asked searching questions. By now I was a little more relaxed and felt confident in the huge strides that we had taken as a college. Some of the financial stresses were easing, although just a little bit. As is the pattern, after a short time we were asked to leave the room and were cloistered in a small, windowless room down the hallway. I warned our trustee that we would be returning to the Commission room in just a short while and to be ready for continued censure.

We waited and waited. Eventually an hour passed, although it seemed like much longer. After about an hour and fifteen minutes the gentleman whom I called "The Sargent" poked his head into the room. His eyes were wide, and he told us that things were happening in the other room such as he had never seen before. He quickly reassured us that it was good rather than bad. A few minutes later he beckoned to us and marched us back before the panel. The atmosphere was completely different. There were smiles. I naturally presumed that they had very good news for us. It was not to be. Once again, we were informed that the probation remained. However, they were so impressed with progress that they had spent the past hour and a bit trawling through the accreditation standards to find ways to help us. They had even produced statements that we could use on our website and in our literature. They explained that, while probation needed to remain, they were sure that there was good cause for them to believe that the future was positive. They stood firm on their standards but gave us much reassurance and encouragement.

At the conclusion of the third year, I made the now familiar journey to appear before the Commission. Still, I was marched in. Still there were a few forthright questions. However, the meeting was much shorter than before, and they assured me that they would not be long in their deliberations. I had hardly found the little room where we were expected to wait before our friend the Sargent beckoned for me enthusiastically. It had only been a matter of a minute or two. I opened the door, and not a thousand guesses would have prepared me for what happened next. I have been told that it had never happened before, but as I entered the room every member of the Commission stood to their feet and applauded as I made my way back to the chair at the front of the room. Some were loudly cheering, several had tears in their eyes. After what seemed like a long time, they took their seats again. Composure was regained and the person appointed as the spokesman began by telling me that he thought that what I had just witnessed said it all. Formally, he went on to tell me that it was with great joy that the Commission had removed all probationary status and that our accreditation was restored completely. What a moment! I wanted to stand on a rooftop somewhere and shout out the good news. All the hard work had paid off. The kindness of many donors was now rewarded. Our carefully constructed programs and degrees enjoyed the endorsement they deserved.

The innovation, affordability and accessibility of Trinity Bible College and Graduate School degrees and programs were now secure into the future. What a faithful God we serve!

CHAPTER SEVEN

Awards and Honors

A Culture of Honor

There are thousands of theories on how best to make a society work. From deep antiquity the philosophers have peddled their thoughts and activists have taken them up, often proving to be more devoted than their teachers. The world seems currently seems to be in a struggle of ideologies on a global scale. Should big government take care of all our needs, or must we demand more of the individual?

This is nothing new, and each generation decides for themselves how they want to be governed. So, the cycles of ideas, successes, failures, violence, and new starts seem to be the lot for the human race. However, we can learn from history, and especially from the biblical record of how God worked in the nation of Israel, that a society that appropriately recognizes achievements and honors the good choices of its citizens works better than those that do not.

A major part of this process is the development of traditions and practices that help to reinforce the good. Thus, the military awards medals, companies give bonuses, and nations honor citizens who have made a notable contribution to the wellbeing of its citizens. Celebrating anniversaries, birthdays and honoring those who have gone on before are all essential components of retaining positive influences in our lives whether at a national or even just a family level.

This is also true of an institution of higher education. Traditions are wholesome, and recognizing high achievement is an essential part of reinforcing the learning process. We can believe that a student graduating this year can do well because we have celebrated an alumnus of the year or other high achieving graduate. We can catalogue the names of our classmates who have worked that little bit extra to make our college experience more rewarding. We can reinforce good memories and speak to future generations of things that are proven and positive.

As our tenure at Trinity got beyond the early survival years, I felt the need to begin some traditions and make awards that would add texture to the College as a whole. It just so happened that, at about the same time as I was beginning to think this way, one of our best-loved and long-serving professors announced his retirement. Professor Warren Schlect was our science instructor. He somehow remembered every student's birthday, knew them all as good friends, and held their attention in the science laboratory. I had never met anyone who did not love Professor Schlect. Our resources were very limited, and I was not sure how best to honor him (and some of his colleagues) as he said his farewell to the classroom. It was not long before years of quiet thought and concepts resulted in the formation of an idea to create an annual award for the teacher of the year and name it in honor of Warren. As we honored him for his years of service it was with great delight that I announced the formation of the "Warren Schlect Teacher of the Year Award." A few years later the Board added an annual cash award to be given to the recipient of this award.

It goes without saying that teaching is a demanding profession. Those who do not make the sacrifices of early studies followed by ongoing professional development are soon found lacking in the classroom. Institutions and administrators work hard to try to prevent teachers from being ineffective. There are regular assessments, classroom reviews and other checks and balances. Finding a standout teacher from the rest is not an easy choice. Future Presidents may use a different process, but I begin early in the spring semester. On-the-spot questions to groups of students standing in the line for lunch can reveal much. Then a quiet question around a coffee in the Commons might reveal what others are thinking. Normally by March or April the choice is made in my mind.

I do all I can to keep my choice secret until the day of graduation. Among all the other things to celebrate on these great days, we always find a time to honor the Teacher of the Year. My fairly informal processes seem to have been accurate. Certainly, judging by the response of the crowd when I make my announcement, I get the feeling that I have got it right. Some make an impression on me because their students are enthusiastically discussing a Bible passage because of a stimulating class. Others quietly excel throughout the year, one recently not only winning the National Coach of the Year award in our athletic division, but also being honored by our own Teacher of the Year award because of his outstanding leadership in athletic and classroom instruction.

Jordan Nowell, Teacher of the Year 2021

Some of the most moving letters ever written to me have come from the recipients of this award. One spoke of her disadvantaged childhood. Almost none of her childhood friends had ever even made it to college, let alone out of high school. And now she was being honored for being an outstanding educator. What a wonderful, redemptive story. I hope that those who come after me will retain the place of the "Warren Schlect Teacher of the Year Award."

In a college such as Trinity a huge emphasis is rightly placed not just on achievement, but on character. Multiple chapel services every week reinforce the place that character plays in our lives, and especially in the lives of those who will become Christian leaders. I wanted to reinforce this emphasis and so the "President's Award" was established. With a deep sense of joy, I approached the Board and then the faculty to propose the establishment of this special award.

Every class seems to have a small group of students that shine a little brighter than the rest. Each year presents people with a different array of gifts, but there are some things that always remain the same among those that become candidates for the President's Award. Perhaps near the very top is a commitment to serve. These are the students that collect their friends' plates to take to the wash up area after a meal. They are the first to volunteer in a campus service day or in our annual "Serve Our City" day.

The diverse group who have received this award over the years also have another strong character trait in place. They are worshippers. This does not mean that they are always active on a worship team or that they are musically skilled. What it does mean is that they are fully engaged. This is especially true in chapel services. After all my years of college leadership it is evident to me within weeks which students might become disengaged or are a high risk in terms of completing their education. Almost always a key factor is a disengaged disposition in chapel services. The "ho hum" boredom of a disinterested student shouts loudly across a chapel.

Recipients of the President's Award are completely different. They are engaged, involved and enthusiastic. Service, worship, and a willing disposition almost always lead to leadership and influence. These are the students that I search out for. Normally by the beginning of the spring semester the list of potential candidates starts to narrow. Some years the choice has been so difficult. Several could easily have been the correct candidate. Eventually the choice is made and, just like the Teacher of the Year Award, the cheers when the name of the recipient is announced indicate that I have generally got it right. It might seem a little dramatic, but one of the high points in the routine of my year is the moment that I get to announce the President's Award. Congratulations to all those who have been worthy recipients. May Trinity continue to see amazing young women and men - like those who have already passed through our halls far into the future.

Every credible academic institution facilitates some form of public lecture. It could be a series over several months or a single lecture once a year. Due to our location, I opted for a single lecture once a year. The development of the concept coincided with the continued growth of the Graduate School at Trinity. As we had developed the graduate degrees from scratch, we had some freedom to introduce several innovations. One was to include a lecture simply called "Global Scholar" as a core course. It afforded us the opportunity to invite a significant and well recognized person in the academic community to deliver a module once a year. We have been very fortunate to recruit some world class professors to teach this module. We then decided that it would be a good idea to ask the invited professor to deliver an annual public lecture in his or her chosen field of expertise.

Continuing my desire to establish some traditions and grow the reputation of Trinity, I set about naming this annual lecture. There were several obvious candidates and families. Trinity has been so fortunate to have had incredibly generous individuals and families who have supported the College throughout the years. Perhaps one of these deserving individuals should be named. After weeks of careful conversation with many, one name emerged.

The name that kept surfacing was Herman G Johnson. He had served as a pioneer pastor in North Dakota many decades earlier and then, as the Assemblies of God took root across the region, he became the first Superintendent of the Dakota District. Back then it included both North and South Dakota, and their leader was a prominent pioneer. About four years before I became the President, Herman Johnson's son Sam Johnson had become very involved at Trinity. He worked tirelessly to raise funds and help the College through some very lean years. In fact, he had been present on the day that we were asked to consider serving at Trinity. I felt a bond with Sam from the very beginning, and he and his precious wife Joyce have been some of our most valued friends. Sam is remarkable in many ways. Energetic, visionary and always inspiring. He is also incredibly generous, not just with money, but with time and in sharing his friends. I will forever be indebted to this incredible Christian leader.

One thing Sam understands better than most is how important it is to trust educators to do their job and to not be overly prescriptive in how to use funds. He excels in his gift of winning the confidence of donors, and then he wisely passes those funds on and entrusts them to the educators. As a result, Sam and his supporters have provided for Bible college education around the world like no one else I know. From the Himalayas to East Africa, and from Europe to Southeast Asia and many other locations around the globe, the ministry of Sam Johnson and Priority 1 is profoundly evident. With this in mind, I approached Sam and asked if he would be open to us naming the public lecture in honor of his father. Sam and his family were jubilant! In fact, most of them traveled to the first Herman G Johnson Lecture and the family has had a presence there every year since.

Although Sam Johnson has consistently expressed his gratitude to me regarding the honor we gave his father, his continued efforts seemed to deserve further recognition. It is not uncommon for Sam to arrive in Ellendale late at night, drive early the next morning to a ranch three hours away, raise some funds, and then return to help level the ground around a new building or pull weeds in a flower bed. Such is the character and caliber of the man. I often felt that my copious "thank you's" were so inadequate. And so it was that I approached our faculty and asked that a process be initiated that would result in the conferral of an honorary doctoral degree on Sam. It involved several committee meetings, careful checks of our accreditation standards and ultimately a vote. It was unanimous. What a day it was when Dr. Sam Johnson entered our chapel to have this highest of honors conferred upon him! He remains one of the most deserving recipients of this kind of award that I have ever known.

With deep satisfaction, I was seeing a culture of tradition, honor and celebration become a part of the fabric of Trinity Bible College and Graduate School. Special alcoves were built into the wall on the corridor leading through to the Prayer Center and large wooden plaques were placed there. Every year it is with joy that I see another name on each of these plaques honoring the achievement of a teacher or an exceptional student. The title and presenter of the "Herman G. Johnson" lecture is also recorded for posterity. Year by year the record of outstanding people is added to, and with it, the culture and richly textured story of Trinity Bible College and Graduate School.

As we concluded our fifth year of service, it came to my attention that one of our Trustees was completing fifty years of service on our Board. Both in the corporate world and the not-for-profit world it is rare to find anyone who has served a company or institution for this length of time. At the time that I became aware of this I did some background research and discovered that the current number of those serving in governance anywhere for fifty years or more numbered no more than fifteen to twenty people. I knew that this special moment in the history of our great college could not go without a very special celebration. The trustee is Silas Liechty. Affectionately known to everyone as Si, this remarkable man and his wonderful wife Martha have been amongst the most generous people I have ever met. It is not uncommon for them to spend large amounts of time during the summer attending events organized by various ministry organizations and they gladly open their hearts and check book on each occasion.

Over the years the Liechtys have given huge amounts of money to Trinity. They seek no attention or even recognition. I have observed Si closely now for nearly ten years. Anyone who aspires to the ministry of giving can learn much from this gracious man. An early lesson that he taught me was to not be afraid to ask affluent people for support. As long as the potential donor knows that he or she can say no to a request, they will never be offended by a forthright appeal. Again, and again this advice has helped me. Another consistent trait of Si is to try to encourage others by his own giving. He will always let others know of his giving in order that they should consider giving as well. He is not always successful in getting others to give even relatively small amounts, but he never ceases from trying to motivate them anyway.

On the occasion of Si's fifty years of service on Trinity's Board, I wanted to honor him and Martha in a special way. But, imagining what that might be was not as easy. Another plaque, card and bouquet of flowers was not going to impress them. Yet, I wanted a way to honor them that would remain as a legacy to their kindness.

I decided to create a special award to be known as the "Silas and Martha Liechty Outstanding Service Award." I submitted the idea to the Board of Trustees (via email in order to not give it away to Si) and everyone enthusiastically agreed. We created this award to honor those who have made a very significant contribution to the growth and development of Trinity. In other words, people who serve with the same spirit that Si and Martha have shown over so many years.

Si & Martha Liechty

As I conceived this new award the first recipient was an obvious choice. Superintendent Leon Freitag had served on the Board for twenty years. For many of those years he had served as Chairman and now he was the Vice-Chair. A more gracious man is hard to meet. Leon and Dianne had been supportive of me from the very beginning. He had opened good doors to me in our early days and had been a constant source of encouragement and insight. Now he was battling mesothelioma and was in constant distress. Yet he bore it with dignity. I thus approached the Board and recommended that Leon be the first recipient of the Si and Martha Liechty Outstanding Service Award. There was unanimous agreement with my recommendation.

It was decided that we should use the annual graduation ceremony as an appropriate time to announce the award and the first recipient. I could hardly wait! It seemed not only the right thing to do but was also a significant development in the reinforcing of our desire for a culture of honor and good tradition. We managed to get the word out to some family members and the graduation began, as it always does, with great celebration and cheering as the graduands make their way into the hall. After early formalities I stood to announce this brand-new initiative. I gave some background and then stated that the new award would be name the Si and Martha Liechty Outstanding Service Award. They were characteristically shocked and humbled. They made their way to the platform with loud cheering taking place throughout the hall. I looked down at their daughter and son-in-law and could not help but catch their radiant faces as they celebrated with us. We had produced a beautiful certificate and I presented them with the framed document as Carol made her way to the platform with some beautiful flowers for Martha. They were taken completely by surprise which made the moment even sweeter for me.

As the cheering died down, I asked Si and Martha to remain with me at the podium. It was then that I announced that the Board had already agreed upon the first recipient. I had deliberately scheduled for Leon Freitag to be the graduation speaker, and I asked Si to announce him as the first recipient. Again, there was loud cheering and Leon seemed completely taken aback. The award was made, amazing people were honored, and I was delighted.

Each year at the fall meeting of the Board of Trustees there is a standing business item. It is a consideration of who might be the next worthy recipient of this prestigious award. To date there has not been a second person recognized but several are certainly worthy, and I am sure the Board will find an appropriate time to honor these individuals. For me, the fact that such an award exists is wonderful.

As Trinity's stature in the academic world rises and more and more people receive their degrees and awards, it warms my heart to know that we have created a strong basis for recognizing more than academic achievement alone. Early pioneers, teachers, outstanding students, and extraordinary friends of the College are all honored and recognized as they should be. I have dreamt of new buildings, helped establish innovative new academic programs and much more in our ten years at Trinity. Yet, almost nothing gives me as much joy as the progress we have made through awards and honors to the building of an institution with rich heritage, great traditions, and a culture of honor.

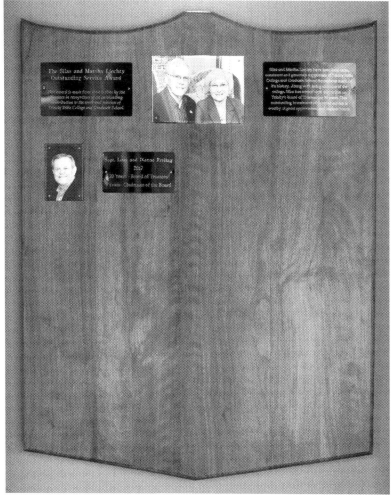

Plaques of Awards hanging in Prayer Chapel.

CHAPTER EIGHT

The President's Council

The President's Council – Advice and Investment

As Carol and I embarked on the journey to Trinity, we had the joy of meeting one of America's most accomplished Christian educators. Dr. Bob Cooley had started his career as an archaeologist and eventually served as the President of one of the most prestigious seminaries in the United States.

His archaeological training had given him an eye for detail which he applied to the important role of those in governance in an institution. He and his lovely wife lived in a retirement complex south of Charlotte, North Carolina. We soon became great friends, and I regularly made the trip to visit him. We would meet at a coffee shop near his home. His favorite pastry was called a "bear claw," and he would devour one each time we met. Bob was a wealth of information on a wide variety of subjects, and each time we met was an enriching experience. I do believe that the feeling was mutual.

Some of the early advice that he gave me was to enlist the

support of influential and affluent people who would not necessarily be well suited to the established role of a Board member. People with wisdom and insight who could give perspective and offer objective advice. The idea was a good one, but how would I find, let alone recruit, people like this? At times it felt as though we had been parachuted into the northern plains, and the lack of long-term friendships and connections was something I was constantly reminded of.

Besides, at the time that we were talking about a council of influential friends, I was trying my utmost to simply get through one week at a time. It had proven difficult to even build a functioning cabinet let alone expand to a group of people that would scrutinize my leadership very closely. The idea of gathering the proposed council seemed to be something for the distant future.

As has been the case on numerous occasions, the power duo of Sam Johnson and Si Liechty helped move things forward. It is hard to overstate the influence of these two amazing men. They both represent a unique blend of vision along with commitment to action. For example, soon after we arrived at Trinity, we left the chapel to find two beautiful people mover vans, two cars and another van all wrapped in Trinity Bible College vinyl decals in the parking lot. Our two friends had arranged and paid for them all. Every institutional leader need people like Sam and Si. Unfortunately, people like these are few and far between. How fortunate we were that they were a part of our team!

They suggested that we plan a meeting to discuss the management structure of the College. A room was booked in a hotel in Jamestown, ND, and several of us met. We reached out to a fine couple who had run a successful business in Minneapolis and asked if they would help guide the conversation. And so, Gordon and Danita Bye entered our lives and began to lead our first meeting. Their advice was invaluable, and soon multiple, creative concepts were being shared. Important steps were taken to help formulate how to structure our internal management in such a way as to move us forward. Eventually the concept of a "President's Council" was proposed.

The idea proposed had many echoes of the advice that my dear friend Bob Cooley had given a few years before. A council of wise friends who would bring both experience and valuable relationships to the table was what we were dreaming of. Multiple pieces of flip chart paper began to line the walls of our small conference room in the Jamestown hotel. More importantly, I felt vision and courage rise in my heart. Ideas flowed freely, and eventually we had a plan moving forward.

Firstly, we felt very strongly that, if married, whoever we invited to join the President's Council should serve as couples. We wanted the wisdom of life, the experience of years and the perspective of godly couples. Then, we wanted to be sure – and I was particularly insistent on this - that the format of each meeting would include careful consultation with the strong commitment to give counsel to the President. This would require the trust of the Board so that their legitimate role was never usurped. The whole idea required great diplomacy and careful communication. We were beginning one of the most enriching journeys of my life as a Christian leader.

Our first meeting was planned, and a dinner event arranged. A faithful group of existing donors was invited, and we enjoyed a good evening together. Carol and I shared our vision, and there was a good response. However, it was nowhere near what I was hoping for. I knew we needed more than some dinner receptions. We needed careful consultation. It also struck me that inviting significant leaders to address our group would help raise the bar of our expectations.

Still feeling the afterglow of our Jamestown meeting, I turned once again to Sam Johnson. Few people have the diplomacy and grace mixed with sheer audacity like Sam. I asked if he would be the Chair of our new team and help gather people together. He quickly and willingly responded. He soon began to write masterful letters to several friends who filled exactly the job description of a Council member. One by one they responded in the affirmative, and we felt as though we had a viable group to get another good start.

We met at Trinity Bible College for our first formal gathering and hosted the event in the Atrium of our brand-new Prayer Center. The event was deliberately planned to coincide with the dedication of the Prayer Center. We had invited Rev. Doug Clay to be the speaker at this special event. He was serving on the National Leadership Team of the AG at the time and is now the General Superintendent. His contribution was outstanding, and the glow around Reuben and Clarice Liechty and their son Richard was enthralling. We celebrated their generosity and rejoiced in the statement that a Prayer Center right in the middle of our campus was making. We also had the joy of hosting David and Barbara Green, the founders of the national arts and crafts chain Hobby Lobby. David addressed the President's Council, and we all felt as though the entire event had cemented a future for this amazing group of godly and wise friends. We eagerly began to plan for our next meeting.

And so, the time comes for me to introduce yet another remarkable couple. Sonny and Mary Schriner have lived in the Black Hills most of their lives. Mary's family had worked on the incredible sculpture of Mount Rushmore. Their beginnings were humble, but hard working. They drove school buses for a living and eventually saved enough to acquire a motel in Hill City, South Dakota.

We have traveled widely, and gladly admit that there are few places in the world as beautiful as the Black Hills of South Dakota. At times the ragged, rocky outcrops look more like an exaggerated artist's canvas than real scenery. The trees are majestic and the long, and at times turbulent, history of the place add a mystique. We love the Black Hills. They are made even more wonderful because of the friendship of Sonny and Mary. These are amongst the most kind and hospitable people in the world.

I approached Sonny to enquire if we could book several rooms for an anticipated President's Council meeting. By this time the Schriners had added another, brand new motel to their holdings. Perched on a ridge as you enter Hill City, it is beautiful in every respect. As well as spacious rooms there are adequate conference facilities, and so the venue was ideal for us.

As is his way, Sonny immediately put a plan into action. By the time we had added everyone up, including some Trinity staff to help with logistics and a special guest, we needed about forty-two rooms. I knew that the cost of so many rooms was going to stretch the College budget, but by now we were already deeply invested in the concept of a President's Council, and it was a need that I had to trust God to meet.

We had invited a passionate pastor friend to be our special guest. Randy Valimont and his wife Jelly pastored a dynamic church in Griffin, Georgia. We had become friends, and Randy willingly committed to join us for a few days in the Black Hills. His various responsibilities including leading a large church, a successful school, and managing a very substantial mission budget, gave him a vocabulary and perspective that was very helpful to us. Sadly, Randy died suddenly a few years ago, but I will forever be indebted to him for inspiring faith at our Council meeting in the Black Hills.

In addition to Randy, we had also extended an invitation to our friends Gordon and Danita Bye who had been so instrumental in helping our thinking some months before. We arrived on a perfect afternoon. Sonny and Mary were wiping tables, helping people find their rooms and serving us sacrificially. It was humbling to see this successful couple being available to us, and nothing was too small for them to not give their personal attention to it.

I have a deep sense that God used Sonny and Mary in a very special way. It was not long before I found out that they had planned to provide the entire two-day event, including meals, at no cost to us. I tried to insist, but Sonny would have nothing of it. We ate at a famous steak restaurant that evening and, when I went to pay the bill, it was already taken care of. The conference rooms were beautifully equipped, and each table was set with an array of refreshments. I was not allowed to pay for a single thing. And then it dawned on me – Sonny and Mary's generosity was a key that was opening something in the unseen world. Somehow, they were providing a breakthrough for us because of their incredible servanthood and generosity.

Randy Valimont inspired us all. He shared several devotions and provoked faith in the group. Then we asked Gordon and Danita to help us. Out came the flip chart paper, searching questions were asked and small groups began to meet around the tables. The level of conversation in the room was incredible. Our decision to invite couples was proving to be the right choice. As I looked around the room, it seemed to me that everyone was absorbed in the conversations. Great ideas were shared. Importantly, this wise group of friends were very honest about the vulnerabilities of Trinity Bible College and Graduate School. Most particularly was the constant mention of our unrealistic debt burden. These were experienced people who had run businesses and succeeded in life. To a person they wanted to see the College become resilient, and a key part of achieving that was to get rid of the debt.

I was torn. Of course, I wanted the debt gone, but I was also aware of the large amount of deferred maintenance that our campus was creaking under. I knew that we need some innovative programming that would cost money. I was constantly reminded of our antiquated IT equipment and slow internet speeds. It was difficult to get a sense of priorities when battling with these daily challenges. But I had to concede that the combined wisdom of the group in that room in the Black Hills far surpassed my own, and I listened intently. My heart was telling me that they were right. My head did not always agree.

What a powerful combination of influence and wisdom was in that room! Again, we filled dozens of sheets with our ideas and thoughts, and the day passed in a buzz of vision, concepts and suggestions. As the day drew to a close, we all knew that we had seen a better future together. There was some natural fatigue as the discussions had been fervent and long, but there was an equal sense of accomplishment. I must admit that I was not sure how to bring the proceedings to a close.

With years of experience and a sensitivity to God's leading, Sam Johnson stepped forward. He did not pause; he knew exactly what to do. With a unique combination of humility and forthrightness he asked the group how they could help meet the goals that had been set that day. He quickly circulated some simple sheets of paper and asked our friends to make some form of a pledge.

I will never forget that moment. For me, it was like all the air was sucked out of the room. Everyone went silent. There was hardly a movement, and my first thought was that we had ruined the whole day by making a financial appeal. I remember turning slightly into the corner near where I sat. The tension, at least to me, felt palpable. Sitting to Sam's right hand side, a couple who had been animated and quite verbal throughout the day suddenly moved, and the gentleman quickly stood to his feet. With the classic forthrightness of a rancher, he said something to the effect that we should all stop messing around, and he slipped a piece of paper into Sam's hand.

Sam quietly looked at the paper, and I thought he was about to collapse. He let out a cry and then began to weep openly. I still had no idea what he had read, but the emotion and the tension of the moment seemed to affect all of us in the room. I shrank further into my little corner and found waves of emotion overtaking me. I still did not really know why. After gaining some composure, Sam finally was able to tell us what he had read. The little note contained a pledge for $1 million! It was restricted to debt reduction, but suddenly the floodgates that had been wedged slightly open by Sonny and Mary's generosity burst open.

Couples gathered where they were, and the room was filed with hushed conversations. Soon, other pledge forms began to make their way to Sam, and he and one or two others began to tally the total. About ten minutes later the big announcement was made. In addition to the initial $1 million another $2.2 million was pledged. Some was restricted for one project or another, but each one spoke of a faithful God who had a future for us at Trinity. We were elated and exhausted all at the same time. The atmosphere was electric. It was a moment that will live with me forever.

Carol and I left the Black Hills the next morning. Again and again, we have seen God meet incredible needs. In one sense this was yet another event to be added to the catalogue of God's faithfulness in our lives. But in another sense, this was different. We felt that this was a reminder that there was still a place for the training of men and women for God's work in our contemporary world. We felt it was a strong affirmation of the assurances Bob Cooley had given years earlier. It reinforced a sense that we had journeyed in faith but were exactly where God wanted us to be.

A year later the President's Council came together in the beautiful western North Dakota town of Medora. Set right on the edge of the magnificent Theodore Roosevelt National Park, the little town is a delight! Roosevelt is celebrated everywhere. Before becoming President, the poor man lost both his wife and mother on the same day. To help overcome his grief he made his way to the far west of North Dakota, and in the rough and tumble world of prairie ranchers he found himself again. The Little Missouri River flows through these unusual lands carving its way slowly south. It was this river that carried Lewis and Clark on their epic journey of discovery that eventually led them all the way to the west coast. On either side of the river are the colorful buttes that form the remarkable badlands of the North Dakota. It is beautiful and brutal all at the same time.

We planned to meet during the day and celebrate by attending the Medora Musical that evening. Before enjoying the musical, we all shared a pitchfork fondue meal. Huge 12-ounce steaks are loaded onto a pitchfork and plunged into a cauldron of boiling oil. They are then served with baked potato and beans on a steel plate reminiscent of what the cowboys would have used. It all contributed to yet another memorable gathering of the President's Council.

Rev Rick du Bose, who now serves as the Assistant General Superintendent, was our guest. Again, there was animated discussion. At times hard questions were asked. The Council was about its business and performing exactly as we had intended. Scrutiny, searching questions, advice and encouragement were all present on this occasion.

By now the Council was enjoying high levels of trust, and Carol and I felt covered and cared for. We felt that we could be vulnerable, open, and transparent. Our meetings became valuable times that we look forward to, then and now.

Subsequent meetings have been as engaging as any of those already described. Major projects became the focus of the Council and on each occasion, there has been a generous response. At the time of writing the entire debt is within sight of being paid off. This will contribute immensely to the resilience of the College in the years to come. A major donation has allowed the complete renovation of our main women's dormitory. Literally thousands of volunteer hours have been given in addition to the initial gift, and the dormitory now boasts new bathrooms, windows, carpets, paint and much more.

President's Council members dedicating Davidson Hall
(Pictured from left to right: Roger & Marilyn Baker, Clarice
& Reuben Liechty, Joyce & Fred Evans, Jon McCreary)

The cafeteria at Trinity had slowly become the least attractive part of our campus. Efforts to improve it were superficial and cosmetic. It was time for a complete refurbishment. Building costs were soaring as the supply chain post COVID took its toll. Nevertheless, our devoted President's Council members took on the challenge. In the Fall of 2021, our students returned to a state of the art, fully refurbished cafeteria.

The list of accomplishments could go on. This gracious team have been the source of immense encouragement to us. Their generosity is incredible! Their wisdom and insight are invaluable. May this short record of their faithfulness serve to inspire future generations of Council members and the wider Trinity community. The bar has been set very high. These remarkable people have transformed our college. To them I give honor and gratitude. To God I give all the glory.

CHAPTER NINE

The Importance of Good Leaders

The Board of Trustees – Leadership and Governance

Please allow me the indulgence of potentially boring you. What I want to write about is a subject near and dear to my heart. It does not include stories of multi-million-dollar donations or other dramatic events. But it is the foundation for all the rest to take place and needs its own space in a book like this.

It is the subject of governance, often referred to in higher education circles as "shared governance." The way in which an institution is led is central to everything - absolutely everything it does.

I had the immense privilege of completing a PhD while serving as the President of the Assemblies of God Bible College and Graduate School. Little had changed there over decades in terms of how the school was governed. A Board of Governors was voted on from time to time at the annual conference of the denomination. My predecessor would often relate nightmare stories of long and unproductive meetings. I did not pay much attention until my PhD studies started to reveal the huge number of seminaries that were closing, or had already been closed, all across America. Almost always there was a constant theme – that of governance.

I began to read further. Again and again, good, well-researched literature highlighted the need for good governance and careful fiduciary management. It seemed as though a common factor in failed institutions was poor governance. There were clear patterns. There was no debate about the obvious need for a governing body. Equally, the expectation of good fiduciary responsibility was not debated. The pattern that emerged was that all too often, the members of the governing body were appointed by some denominational group and were not as personally invested as they should be. Then the administration felt that the board was not supportive or did not understand what needed to be prioritized. This tension resulted in relatively short tenures for presidents, and the institution suffered as a result. In recent years the average tenure for a college president is only about six years.

This pattern seemed even more intense for institutions that are faith-based. The complexities of leading such institutions are multiplied several times over. The expectation of the constituency is often unrealistic, and the lack of endowment funds and the pressure of maintaining a strong confessional atmosphere combine to make faith-based institutions particularly vulnerable. Every year I receive notification of another faith-based institution closing its doors forever. Some of these colleges have been around for decades and then close with very short notice. Some accreditors and even government agencies are concerned about this and are raising their expectations for institutions to prove that they are sustainable.

This cauldron of pressure and expectation results in many places of Christian higher education becoming extremely vulnerable. So, what is the solution? Although the answer to this question is obviously textured, I would like to suggest that very near the top of the list is the "ownership" of the college or university. A Board of Trustees is not some disengaged watch dog group that shows up twice a year to check on what is going on. Boards, whatever we call them, are in fact owners. They are the final authority in an institution. So, it stands to reason that good leadership is central to the long-term flourishing of a college or university.

My studies had alerted me, and my own experience had reminded me of this important reality. An institution of higher education can only fly as high as its governance. It is no wonder then, that this became a particular focus of mine when I was asked to lead Trinity Bible College.

I was impressed by our Board. As I got to know them, I found kind and gracious people. Some were particularly inquisitive as to why I had taken the risk of being prepared to serve a school that was in such a vulnerable place. Others watched from a distance. No one was insensitive or unkind. So, we got off to a good start. A few resigned within a month or two. I think they did so with some relief. Our meetings proceeded well, but there was little structure and all that we really did was consider some reports and then agonize over the finances.

It was also evident that we were a relatively homogenous group. Nearly everyone was male, most were clergy, and the majority were at least middle aged. We had no Board committees, no means of monitoring how long anyone had served, and few knew how best they could serve the College. It was not their fault. One generation of trustees had morphed into the next without much thought or strategy. I knew it was time for change.

I requested that I be given time for a brief seminar in one of our earliest meetings. I chose as my subject the importance of fiduciary responsibility. This is a term that is often bandied about, but I wondered how many really understood what it meant. At its heart, "fiduciary" not only means that an institution is governed within the requirements of the law but goes further. It requires a board to demonstrate that both the legal requirements governing an institution are met and that the intent of the constituency is fulfilled as well. In other words, if a college contracts with its students through the publishing of a catalogue, then it is ultimately the board's responsibility to ensure that this contract is adequately carried out. If courses are not being taught or papers are not being effectively graded, the Board should know. Likewise, if a donor gives money, it is the board's responsibility to ensure that those funds are used as intended. This means that they cannot be used in the pursuit of another priority; they must be used carefully and accurately according to the wish of the donor. Thus, intent is as important as legality.

I remember finishing my twenty-minute presentation and sat down. The Board secretary was the first to speak up. He said, "Now you have scared the daylights out of us!" I expressed my satisfaction. That is exactly what I had intended. If our College was to flourish, it would require the determined commitment of the Board to fully carry out its fiduciary responsibilities. Some asked what the next steps were, and, by the end of our meeting, I felt empowered to bring change and new direction.

We began by ensuring that we identified the core work processes of the College. From these we worked upwards including every employee in the process. At times it was challenging. Colleges are complex and presenting them schematically is not easy. In a place like Trinity, it is even more difficult. Many people have to multi-task for our resources to stretch far enough. But, a pattern emerged, internal management systems were established, and our great College began to become functional.

Board committees were formed to reflect these core work processes. It was fascinating to see these dedicated people get down to a detailed level of involvement in all that mattered to the business of the College. Each committee was formed with a clear statement of its responsibility and function. A template was created by which meaningful feedback could be brought to the full Board meeting.

I soon realized that I did not have either the time or the organizational capacity to ensure that the Board functioned as we intended for it to. We had good documents, a good structure, and some clearly defined roles, but I needed more. I needed to ensure that we "played by our own rules." I wanted to avoid the challenge of recurring business that can hinder the effectiveness of a board. I needed a Board of Trustees mentor.

Just a little time before we had welcomed back an old friend of the College to serve on the faculty. David Bennett had an exemplary record of service over many years at Trinity. He had worked hard to achieve a doctoral degree and over the years had served several churches and ministries. After receiving a generous grant to develop a BA degree linked to a MA degree enabling hard-working students to graduate with both degrees in just five years, the obvious choice of a leader for this program was Dave. We called the program the "Accelerate degree program" and now, five years later our choice of Dave has been confirmed again and again.

Although he was obviously busy with the academic responsibilities we had given him, I approached Dave about serving as our Governance Mentor. He immediately responded positively. We agreed to scour through all our documents, check previous minutes and ensure that there was total transparency in all our meetings. No one could be better suited to the role of Governance Mentor than Dave. Meticulous, careful, organized and overflowing with kindness and grace, he has put his stamp firmly on the affairs of the Trinity Board of Trustees.

He makes sure that information is readily available. Our trustees can be assured of excellent record keeping, and his regular notes fill in the important business with little narratives of things happening around campus. It all combines to reassure our constituency – accreditors, auditors, donors, students, and alumni that Trinity takes good governance and effective leadership seriously.

From the early beginnings of reorganizing the Board of Trustees, things have continued to develop. I gained the confidence to begin inviting highly qualified people to serve. I knew their experience would be a good one. We now have a medical specialist, a state legislator, a corporate attorney, and a Native American leader serving on our Board. The number of women on the Board is increasing, and slowly there is a growing racial diversity as well.

Personally, Board meetings are a highlight of my year. I enjoy welcoming this qualified, diverse, and godly group to the campus each spring and fall. Our meetings are rigorous, thorough, and always edifying. We encourage spouses to attend, and Carol makes sure that there is always a special treat for the women who are there. We always eat together, engage the wider campus community as much as we can and enjoy the few days.

Board of Trustees

Unwittingly, I started a tradition that now serves us well. In the early days there was no budget for special times like a Christmas celebration for staff and faculty. In one of our meetings, I reached out to the Board to ask for their help. There was no budget available for a Christmas party or for small gifts for the whole team. Sam Johnson seized the moment and began tearing a sheet of paper into small sheets. He asked every Board member to indicate what they would do to help me in this appeal. Wonderfully, the amount pledged provided for a special Christmas celebration. Carol and I traveled to Fargo and filled our vehicle with gifts and goodies. Carol baked for days, and we enjoyed our first "President's Christmas Tea." The tradition has continued.

At the next meeting I related my desire to provide an outstanding startup event for staff and faculty. We called it "Vision Day." Again, Sam passed around little squares of paper. Again, they were collected, and the total amount pledged announced. It was a marvelous sum, enough for a sumptuous catered meal, door prizes and more. In recent years one very generous member of the Board has provided two nights in a beautiful Black Hills hotel with a cash allowance for travel and meals as a prize. Several of our team have enjoyed this generous gift.

Good fiscal discipline, careful planning, much communication, and small traditions all combine to remind our wider constituency that Trinity is here to stay. It has a good future; it is in good hands. Good leadership makes for a good College, and we are determined to keep building on the progress already made. I commend our Board of Trustees to all who read this.

CHAPTER TEN

The Case for Campus Based Higher Education

The current group of high school and college age students are the first in several generations to have lived through a world-wide pandemic. In fact, this generation has had to deal with a phenomenon never ever experienced in the history of the world. With gigantic communication networks and enterprises spanning the globe, the onset of a pandemic took on proportions that human beings have not had to deal with before.

Although there is still much to be understood coming out of the pandemic, some of which might take decades to fathom rather than years, the "new normal" remains a mystery to most. Sadly, the divisive political influences that have fueled so much speculation and fear have insidiously invaded almost every area of life. Understandably there is a hesitance on behalf of students and their families alike when it comes to making choices about how to get a quality education and where.

One of the narratives that has been somewhat entrenched because of this global upheaval is that going to college for several years is not economical and, just like having the convenience of home delivery, gaining an education should be the same. Generally, colleges have responded to this narrative and huge investments have been made in online programs and virtual campuses.

As an educator some of these trends seem troubling for me. There are simply no long-term studies that show what social or phycological impact an education that takes place outside of community might have. So, at best, both sides of the argument are left having to speculate. So, in the absence of hard or persuasive data I find myself doing two things. Firstly, I try to understand the biblical narrative and its overarching message. Secondly, I lean into primitive understandings of personhood. Let's start with the first.

Apart from the first few verses of the creation narrative, the first Bible story related to man is the creation of a companion. God saw that it was not good for Adam to be alone and so he created a helpmeet, a friend, a companion, and a mate. Deeply engraved in the foundation of the biblical narrative is the creative purpose of God for human beings to be in communion with Him and with each other.

What follows this most ancient of stories is a very clear blueprint for humanity. Put simply it is family or community. The calling of God's ancient people to be the bearers of a redemptive message for all humanity is always based upon the inter-generational transmission of faith. From Abraham to Isaac. From Isaac to Jacob and then on through the sons of Jacob. Again, and again the Bible speaks of teaching the next generation. Special days, holy days, rituals, and routines are established through the unfolding of the biblical story all with one purpose – to establish a clear and obvious transmission of faith and values.

Jesus chose to entrust His most remarkable of all redemptive stories to a team. He lived His life within a community. The pattern was followed very explicitly by the primitive church and most of the New Testament is written to gathered communities of believers. It is very difficult to read the Bible and not be aware of the consistency of the importance of community.

Sociologically the same is true. Virtually every archeological dig that has ever taken place layers back the life of communities. People function together and bring the diversity of their skills and talents to play for the benefit of the greater whole. Butchers and bakers, tradesmen and merchants all form a part of the textured story of any ancient city or culture. Clans and tribes form. Nations coalesce and each successive generation seeks to find ways for the community as a whole to live better. From laws and culture to water systems and engineering the goal is all the same. It is to facilitate and accommodate community.

I tend to believe that the safest place to live out our lives is within the confines and benefits of a community. It is here that we learn practices and customs that, although they mutate over time, have generally served to create responsible citizens and productive individuals. Denying the benefits of being a part of a community is a very hard proposition to try to defend. It simply has no verifiable evidence. We are wired, created to live, and serve in community.

What is true as we read the biblical narrative and then equally true as we examine the progression of human society over vast periods of time is community and belonging are central to our existence. I contend that the same is true for learning and education.

Nearly 1000 years of formal education starting with the University of Paris in the 13th Century, seems to confirm my persuasion that learning is best undertaken within a community. In fact, all the ancient universities consisted of colleges. These were smaller communities made up of scholars and learners, mentors, and friends. A visit to Oxford or Cambridge will quickly make the visitor aware of these ancient institutions. It was in the college, not the classroom, that the greater part of a student's education took place. This was where they were held accountable, where they learnt tradition, where they were mentored on a daily basis. They ate together, learnt the skill of debate and critical thought, and eventually graduated with a degree that ensured that they knew their subject well. No other social construct in the world has been so successful in training and developing sharp minds. It is this system that was the seedbed for Isaac Newton to learn about gravity or for Einstein to propose his theory of relativity. It was this system in Scotland that proposed the idea of "common sense" and wrote literature that would find its way into world transforming documents such as the American Declaration of Independence and the US Constitution.

What was true for the sciences, philosophy and law is equally true of the arts. Gracious conservatoriums were built in Vienna, Paris, London and eventually New York and Philadelphia. Schools of music and drama produced the performers that would entrance millions with their brilliance. Famous dance companies were established from Moscow to Dublin and subsequently throughout the new world.

Oh, and this is equally true for theological education. Building on a strong tradition of learning established in ancient Greece as well as a pharisaic model used over centuries in the Jewish community, Origen in Jerusalem and other members of the group of ancient church fathers that we call the patristics taught theology and Christian thought using the tradition of learning within the community. Augustine in particular wrote specifically about the academy as a community. Monasteries and academies ensured a steady supply of men for the work of the church. Then came the universities that continued the tradition of the campus. Some of the most elegant ancient buildings in the world today are the cloistered structures of ancient centers of learning. The Reformation that took place over 500 years ago greatly valued education and insisted on a systematic education for all who would serve as pastors and ministers.

The vibrant faith that characterized early generations of Americans was served by the establishment of communities of learning. Starting with the University of William and Mary in Williamsburg, Virginia and followed soon after by Harvard and Yale the deepest of the roots of some of the greatest universities in America go into the soil of a commitment to community.

So why, in the early 21st Century are we struggling to embrace the importance of a campus and community-based education? The answer is complex and textured, but I would like to suggest some of the trends that have led to the undervaluing of a campus-based education.

Very few things happen rapidly when it comes to assessing human behavior. It is this slow shift that we often refer to as cultural change. Small mutations, changing ideas and sometimes epic events all combine over time to create the culture that we live and work in. At times this shift is almost imperceptible, but the march of time brings with it multiple changes. Within a generation or two values change and then attitudes, and behaviors change too. At other times it might only take half a generation to produce significant change in attitudes, values, and behaviors. For example, the development of effective and easily accessible birth control for women in the early sixties produced what we often refer to as the sexual revolution. This quickly developed and was compounded by the anti-establishment forces that were reacting to the ongoing Vietnam war. It was not long before these significant forces coalesced into a free love, anti-authority culture that remains with us to this day. Importantly, these cultural shifts have also impacted Christian higher education and ministry education in particular.

Adding courses from the broader humanities curriculum, employing larger number of professors who had received their education in secular institutions with no biblical content at all and the need to increase tuition rates to sustain these trends tended towards the diminishing of the distinction between a Christian higher education and that received in a community college or secular university. Culture and social pressures were slowly and, at times, insidiously eroding the role of and the distinctives of Christian education in general and perhaps most significantly, the ministry training institution.

The context that I have just described naturally flows into another force that has eroded our commitment to a campus-based education. It is the undergirding pillars of higher education itself. For several hundred years following the Reformation the fundamental structures and goals of the university system remained relatively consistent. The importance of a faith-based education in a campus community was seldom questioned in the heady days of colonial America. Reading the student handbook of Harvard University in the mid 18th century would raise a hearty amen from any Christ-follower today. But slowly Aristotelian views were resurgent and began to take root in the university system. The natural world became the center of academic pursuit and botanists and those developing the early systems of biology started to become strong driving forces in the development of universities.

By the end of the 19th Century Darwinian views dominated and a category of study broadly called the "humanities" took over the curriculum. This resulted in the growth of an entire part of the education system that we also often refer to as the "social sciences". There were obvious advantages to these educational developments. New medicines were discovered such as penicillin for example. It was impossible to gainsay the advantages of the progress of learning. Inevitably resources flowed towards the new sciences and slowly the arts became the poor cousins of the university campus. Over years this trend has compounded and a narrative that a Christian higher education on a campus that holds fast to a Christian world view is not necessarily a good investment. Unfortunately, the response of those involved in Christian higher educational was not always constructive. Like many institutions before, the 20th Century has seen hundreds of thoroughly Christian institutions lose their distinctive. As a result, they have attracted more students often to the detriment of those institutions that seek to retain a strong, community-based confessional position. The distinctly Christian university in the United States is now a threatened entity. Even more so the institution primarily committed to ministry training.

Let me mention one additional force in the erosion of campus-based Christian education. It is the contemporary church. Over time the wider church has played less and less a role in education. Only a few generations ago church leaders were key leaders in universities. As a result, it was almost without question that those of faith believed in educating the next generation. Progressively there has been a development of a disconnect between church and education. It could be argued that the significant growth of Christian schools based in local churches is a counter argument to this view. I concede it is but only to a very small degree. I meet very few church leaders who would have in any way a developed theology of higher education. A surprisingly large number actually hold strong anti-intellectual views and generalize that all education is left leaning and corrosive to faith. I could expand this point at length but suffice it to say that it not difficult to show multiple trends over the twentieth century that are evidence of church leaders losing confidence in higher education. Understandably the secularization of education generally is perceived as a threat to the spiritual aspirations that church leaders have for their congregations.

However, we assess these forces, they have combined to produce cynicism and suspicion of higher education by Christians generally. Now, add the awful onslaught of COVID-19 and the massive growth of online education offerings and the campus-based education valued by so many up until now is under great threat. A narrative that combines the convenience of web-based learning, the questionable benefits of a community context and the high cost of campus-based education all conspire to make the college campus a threatened entity.

I am hoping that this book and this chapter will help reverse this trend. Why might you ask? Well, going back to how this chapter started, it is simply because we need community as people and learning is much more than taking courses. Actually, I am passionate about a residential education. Surgeons have to spend time dissecting cadavers. Engineers have to work in their respective laboratories. Pilots must fly planes in order to get a license. It is simply not conceivable that we can learn everything through a remote learning method. Neither should we. What is true for the vast number of professions is even more critical for Christian higher education. It is in the community that lasting values are learnt and the importance of faith is transmitted.

So, what is the remedy? Firstly, it is that everyone reading this book at least join the debate. I know this is a complex issue for us to work through. I know that there are many good reasons why the campus-based education and training that I am advocating is being questioned. However, it is irresponsible for any generation to unnecessarily condemn the next generation to the consequences of decisions taken without careful consideration. It is that consideration that I am calling for.

Then, get involved in education. If you have younger children go to school board meetings. See what is being taught. Ask your church leaders what they are doing about their own educational journey. Are they upskilling in a way that will equip them to meaningfully engage a changing culture? Research opportunities for your student early and carefully. How will they mature into responsible citizens, not merely get courses completed?

My hope is that you will come to appreciate the benefits of training and education within the context of a community. By that I mean campus-based education. If so, save intentionally for your own students' education and if possible, for that of your grandchildren.

If you are a person that is able to contribute towards charitable causes, I would ask you to investigate the virtues of contributing towards Christian higher education. Do not overlook the need for bricks and mortar. A carpenter needs the tools of the trade, as does a builder. An educator needs a classroom, a great IT system and comfortable dormitories and cafeteria.

Despite all that I have written perhaps my single biggest reason for believing in campus-based education is a small institution in the middle of the North American prairies called Trinity Bible

College and Graduate School. On the surface there seems to be no compelling reason why this institution should exist. The town is small, the region relatively sparsely populated. Would this not be an ideal test case for remote learning? Why develop a campus and then try to motivate young people to move to a place where Walmart is a forty-five-minute drive away? There is one reason – community. It is here that students grow social graces and interreact with one another. It is here that mature Christian leaders spend intensives in classes that open their eyes to engaging better with their culture. I have simply seen life transformation take place on our campus far too often not to passionately believe in the value of the campus.

Several years ago, we hosted a team of volunteers from Virginia. Coming to Ellendale was like a major mission trip for them. They were enthralled. How did people live in a remote setting like this? It was summer so the weather was mild. Some would go out and lie on the bleachers that lined our football field and gaze in wonder at a night sky unspoiled by urban lights.

One day, after a busy time of painting and cleaning they finished dinner together. They were obviously tired, but they were feeling the summer heat. One of the groups commented on how nice it would be to spend some time in a cool mall. This seemed like a great idea and asked our project manager if he could arrange a visit to the local mall. They were amazed when he told them we did not have one. The looks of disbelief were everywhere. They then wanted to know what students did when they just wanted to "hang out". The answer was simple. They went to the local Cenex gas station. After all they served reasonable pizza there and it was convenient. Still with a degree of disbelief the group asked if they could go to the Cenex station. And so they went, bought some pizza and ice cream, and had the time of their lives. Facebook posts were sent around the country. The reality was that they were enjoying what they were created to enjoy. They were enjoying community, exactly as Trinity students do.

It is this community that makes our graduates hardy and

courageous. As a time of lock down began in the early months of COVID I remember looking across the lawns from our house and there were students spontaneously holding a worship service. I see them week after week working through issues in our vibrant chapel times. I look at future schoolteachers standing in quiet submission to the will of God at the front of our chapel and think to myself how fortunate a community will be to have people like this teach in their local school.

Graduation Spring 2021

Then there are the "GO Trips" when students travel in teams. Books could be written of the incredible experiences they share together. New cultures, different languages, travel delays and strange food all combine to provide maturity and spiritual growth in ways that can be found nowhere else. Eating a guinea pig in Peru, trekking through the Himalayas in northern India, serving in Dream Centers in Las Vegas and Los Angeles – these are all experiences that only the commitment to learning in community can provide.

I have watched in awe as our Pack Your Bags students start their year of adventure with team building exercises. Then they travel to Milwaukee and spend twenty-four hours in poverty simulation living on the streets. Their lives are transformed for the better.

I quietly walk through our cafeteria and there, day after day, are dedicated professors taking another half an hour or more to engage in some lively conversation with eager students. These moments are inestimable in their value and impact.

At times I drive slowly along Main Street. I see retail outlets that have shut their doors. I see the lasting impact of relative poverty in small town and rural America. Of course, I know that this kind of hardship is not restricted to our rural communities. Thousands of urban areas are blighted with crime, poverty and violence. As the cold fingers of heartache and despair rise in my heart when surveying these realities, I get to the intersection of Main Street and 6th Avenue South. There before me is the campus of Trinity Bible College and Graduate School. Now fully restored, this vista fills my heart with courage. It is on this quiet campus and in these hallowed halls that the bravest missionaries are being trained. It is here that young men and women are feeling the confirmation of their call to serve as youth pastors and to lead new churches. It is here that the most creative and courageous generation of schoolteachers are receiving their education. Here, in this monastic space set in the windswept prairies is hope for this nation and beyond. This is why I believe in campus-based training and education.

Please join this noble cause. Trust with me for Christian higher education everywhere. Believe with me for the sustaining of learning and thinking communities that are deeply committed to the Bible, who have a well-developed Christian worldview and are determined to pass the baton to another generation of people that will take this Good News of a loving and compassionate Jesus into all the world.

CHAPTER ELEVEN

Onwards and Forwards

I tend towards optimism. Perhaps it was just the way that I was raised or the good schooling I received for which I am very grateful. But, on reflection, I think there are more substantial reasons.

As global pilgrims, Carol and I have had to exercise faith again and again. Over two decades ago we moved from Australia to the US to start an entirely new ministry adventure. Our children were both beginning university within weeks of us arriving in our new homeland. We had packed all our earthly belongings into a container, and we were anxiously awaiting its arrival so that Anna and Jay would at least have more than a single change of clothes.

There was great excitement as the truck drove up the long driveway to the home that had been loaned to us by a church in the western suburbs of Chicago. They offloaded the container; I signed the delivery note and we went to open the doors at the rear. It seemed strange to me that there was no seal on the handles. As I pushed the levers up and opened the doors a mattress fell out and it was all I could to avoid having it land on my head. We quickly discovered that, somewhere in transit, our container had been broken into. Every box had been roughly opened. In fact, the boot marks where they had been kicked open were clear. Treasured photo albums had been thrown across the container, most of our clothes were gone and many of our household items damaged beyond repair.

It was not the first time that our children had had all their clothes stolen. Living in rural southern Africa was somewhat dangerous and our house was broken into numerous times. I remember looking anxiously out of the container doors to see Carol's reaction and that of the children. They quietly accepted the situation without complaint. There was a closet in the church where things were collected to help missionary families. We found coats for both Anna and Jay, packed all their belongings into a suitcase and that same day left the container on our driveway and headed to college with them.

They were both fine. After several months they had the things they needed and so did we. We learned that things don't really matter as much as we would tend to think. God was good to us; life went on and we had each other. I guess it is these experiences and many like them that make me an optimist.

Rural America can be a tough place to live and work. Small towns struggle with declining economies and changing employment. Our little town of Ellendale has lost several businesses in our time. A thriving bakery has gone, as has a delightful variety store. An assembly plant closed its doors, and what was once a thriving restaurant was so badly maintained that its beautiful Art Deco building had to be demolished. Our story is true for many small communities across the United States.

So, it is completely legitimate to ask how a small college set in a very small town can hope to have a prosperous future. Added to the geographical challenges facing a college in a rural setting, there are mountains of regulatory and educational changes as well. During the 1960's numerous acts were passed by Congress such as Title IX and Title IV which most are familiar with. These various pieces of legislation were intended to help the country navigate through the upheavals of the civil rights movement and have generally served higher education well. However, as seems to be inevitable, the meanings of words change, and society mutates. As a result, the application of these laws changes as well. The effort to level the playing field for women in the 1960's now seeks to do the same for people who identify with a whole range of gender identities. Some of these mutations in societal views and values are not compatible with people of deep faith who believe that the Bible and Christian tradition dictate their view of morality. It seems more than likely that the culture and faith are going to clash, and, in many ways, this has already happened. This will make things complicated for faith-based colleges and universities.

Yet, I am optimistic. I believe we can maintain our faith and deliver an outstanding education at the same time. During the course of writing this book Trinity Bible College and Graduate School was assisted by an extraordinary group of donors to retire all our debt while, at the same time, completing a multi-million-dollar renovation and refurbishment program across the campus. Just as importantly, our student body has changed over time and now consists of a mature group of Christ-following men and women who, overall, seem clear regarding their vocational calling. Chapel services are vibrant, annual mission trips see students scatter across the earth and employment opportunities are wide open to Trinity graduates. This all combines to fill my heart with courage.

Concurrently with all these developments, we have fully engaged the concept of shared governance. Our Board is more diverse than ever. The most amazing people of faith drawn from a wide variety of backgrounds and occupations populate our Board of Trustees' committees and take care of their ownership and stewardship of the College. These factors and many others lead me to believe with great confidence that Trinity Bible College and Graduate School has a great future.

Allow me to share my understanding of a little of what that future looks like. Without hesitation our mission to be a Bible

College must be at the top of our vision for the next five years and beyond. This means an uncompromising commitment to the Bible. Maybe this sounds a little obvious, but a review of theological education over the past fifty years suggests otherwise. As soon as the Bible becomes an object for study instead of a guide for life its message becomes eroded, and its life-changing narrative loses its power. I will earnestly provide leadership that will ensure a careful reading of the Bible and the deeply held belief that this amazing book with all its component parts is the inspired Word of God.

The chief end of a Bible College is to train men and women to serve God and His church. This too is central to the future of Trinity Bible College and Graduate School. Ministry in contemporary society is complex and challenging. I eagerly anticipate finding innovative ways to train and equip people who can meet these challenges. Let me dream about just a few.

"NextGen" ministry preparedness takes the specific needs of children, young people, and emerging adults very seriously. Many families will choose the church they attend based largely on the provision that is made for their children and young people. Central to the health of a local church is a clear commitment to care for children and youth. At Trinity, we will refuse to believe that a few willing volunteers on a monthly roster are all it takes to run a meaningful ministry for the next generation. Specialized training, academic majors, and significant opportunities to learn from those who are achieving in these areas must be a big part of our future. I envision a "NextGen" major which accommodates multiple internships, relevant intensives and has an engaged faculty. Specializations in children's ministry, youth ministry and emerging adult ministry (sometimes referred to as college ministry) will need to be resourced. Whatever it eventually looks like, I will give my best attention to ensuring that Trinity provides the finest learning environment and opportunities for NextGen pastors and leaders.

Another passion of my heart is to provide the very best facilities and learning for those committed to music and worship ministry.

A worship/music major with voice and instrumental tracks often fills my imagination. Worship team coaching, vibrant and theologically sound songwriting should emerge from dedicated and godly students in this major. Many revivals that have enjoyed long-term impact have had great music and songwriting associated with them. Why should Trinity not be a seedbed of new music and prophetic song?

Please keep dreaming with me. Biblical preaching, both as a calling and as an art, should be prominent in our offerings. Persuasive, carefully constructed, and passionately delivered sermons should be the expectation of every congregation that has a Trinity alumnus serving it. This would require growing our capacity to teach biblical languages, instructing church history more thoroughly and continuing our current strengths of theological learning.

Missionary training with language learning opportunities, cross-cultural communication skills and how to raise and appropriate funds are in this dream. Since I am baring my heart, let me go all the way. Trinity should and hopefully will make a huge contribution to filling the empty pulpits in our land. Yet, my dream is that for every pastor trained and placed in a local church there would be a missionary raised up and sent to distant shores and lost people. Conversations are taking place regarding ministry training for those who would serve in Hispanic communities. The needs of young leaders from the Native American community are working their way into strategic planning. The same is true for training those who minister to the deaf. A major for those committed to compassion ministry is already functioning, and the early developments of a psychology major with pathways to clinical counselling are already underway.

Then there are the "compatible disciplines." I coined this phrase in the early years of my presidency. I reasoned that if we were to be unashamedly a Bible College then we needed a very good rationale for majors that were not, on the surface, ministry-related areas.

Just a few that fill our dreams would be a significant opportunity to train for a vast range of careers in compassion and care services around the world, as well as working within social services and community development initiatives within the US. Certification in teaching English as a second language, integrating a biblical worldview into teaching and similar areas should be available.

A vibrant and innovative teacher education program is highly compatible with a vision for a Bible College. It is hard to imagine a bigger mission field than the schools of the United States. I say this for two primary reasons. The first is the glaring need. Most rural communities find it difficult to recruit teachers and many schools are understaffed. A cursory piece of research will show any concerned person the needs that exist. Many classes are taught by teachers' aides who might have no formal qualifications at all. The second reason is even more compelling. Our schools have become ideological battlegrounds. Everything from gender studies to Critical Race Theory are being introduced into the curriculum in the earliest grades. Parents have been systematically excluded from any say on how their children should be educated. Any young parent must be deeply concerned about the future education of their child.

Combine the immense shortage of teachers with the ideological battles being waged and a powerful Kingdom opportunity presents itself. It is the training of young men and women who gain the best possible education while sitting in vibrant chapel services four times a week. It is in these services that values, choices, morals, and a biblical worldview are secured. Trinity Bible College and Graduate School simply must respond by providing a growing and well-resourced teacher education opportunity. Currently, the facilities that house the teacher education program are undergoing a huge renovation. It is exciting; but also points to the time when these facilities will be quickly outgrown, and more facilities will be required. Early childhood development training should clearly be on the agenda and eventually specialties like special needs training should be included.

Our teacher education program should become the focus of legacy giving. Apart from vibrant local churches in every community, the next most sustainable way of leaving a legacy is to financially support the next generation of student teachers, especially those with a clear commitment to Christ and His Kingdom.

I hope that I am successfully painting a picture of the future of Trinity Bible College and Graduate School. Join with me in adding to the color palette the rich tones of Christian athletics, music and drama presentations, and community service.

Oh, and please do not forget Pack Your Bags! After multiple years of operation this amazing precollege program continues to prove its worth. Designed primarily to help young adults navigate from school to their adult years, Pack Your Bags is a leader in its field.

As boldly as I can let me say it again – Trinity Bible College and Graduate School has a bright and blessed future. Pray with me that hundreds of young men and women will be drawn to the quiet space of the prairies, to a small town with a dynamic college situated on its eastern edge. This is Trinity. Tinged each morning by the bright rays of a rising sun and bathed in the late afternoon by the lingering reds and purples of some of the most dramatic sunsets anywhere on the planet, this place still stands. It is a bold defiance to the ordinary. It refuses to concede any ground to secular culture or antagonist ideologies. It trains men and women with deep theological reflection. It breathes a missional passion, and it is determined to be a part of the rising army of the meek that will carry God's good news around the world and demonstrate, through acts of generous kindness, the love of Christ.

Davidson Hall

Printed in the United States
by Baker & Taylor Publisher Services